CREATI
YOUR EXPERIENCES

A GUIDE TO DISCOVERING AND USING THE BELIEFS THAT DETERMINE THE NATURE OF YOUR LIVING EXPERIENCES

Julian Tytherleigh

"Errors, like Straws, upon the surface flow;
Those who would search for Pearls must dive below..."

John Dryden (1631-1700)

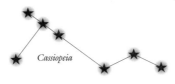

Cassiopeia

SEVEN STARS PUBLISHING

Production management and editorial by Fil Madden

Cover illustration, interior design and film by MacAce, PL27 6HB
Print by Penwell Ltd, Callington, Cornwall PL17 8ER

FURTHER COPIES OF THIS BOOK ARE AVAILABLE FROM

Seven Stars Publishing, 2 The Esplanade, The Hoe,
Plymouth PL1 2PJ; phone and fax 01752 269555

Please contact us for ordering details.

CONTENTS

viii   FOREWORD

x   ACKNOWLEDGMENTS

xi   INTRODUCTION

xiii   USING THIS BOOK

SECTION 1   ESSENTIAL CONCEPTS

1.1   THOUGHTS AND BELIEFS
1.2   HAVING THE POWER TO CREATE, OR NOT?
1.3   BEING SOURCE AND CREATING YOUR EXPERIENCES
1.4   FOCUS AND ATTENTION

SECTION 2   THE THEORY AND REALITY OF BELIEF

2.1   A THEORY OF BELIEFS
2.2   A GUIDE TO DIFFERENT TYPES OF BELIEF
2.3   HOW BELIEFS FUNCTION
2.4   BELIEF PATTERNS, STRUCTURES AND STRENGTH
2.5   BELIEF VARIABLES
2.6   PRESENT TIME, PAST AND FUTURE
2.7   THE EXPERIENCE OF REALITY
2.8   CREATING EXPERIENCES WITH BELIEFS
2.9   CHANGING BELIEFS

Section 3   Self-beliefs and identity

3.1	Self-beliefs and identity
3.2	Self-esteem
3.3	Self-confidence
3.4	Self-worth
3.5	Self-acceptance and self-love

Section 4   Discovering and examining your own beliefs

4.1	Truth and honesty
4.2	What is really important to you - and why?
4.3	Everyday functional beliefs
4.4	Hidden and invisible beliefs
4.5	Belief counselling approaches
4.6	Beliefs, feelings, values and attitudes
4.7	Aliveness and well-being beliefs
4.8	Short-term and long-term beliefs
4.9	Genetic, cultural and group beliefs
4.10	Allowances and other beliefs

Section 5   New possibilities - creating your future

5.1	Choosing your own goals and dreams
5.2	Aligning your goals and beliefs
5.3	Simple techniques to assist you in creating what you want

Section 6 Themes to consider

6.1   Happiness and fulfilment
6.2   Love and relationships
6.3   Money, work and career
6.4   Welfare, health and environment

Section 7 Conclusion and review

7.1   Conclusion
7.2   Review of key insights
7.3   Suggested additional reading
7.4   Some further recommendations of things to do

About the Author

Julian Tytherleigh has a Combined Honours Degree in Social Sciences (politics, economics and sociology) from the University of Plymouth. For the past ten years he has developed a specialised interest in training, counselling and education. He has worked in a training centre, conducting long-term research, and has taught his own adult education courses on beliefs and experience.

He acknowledges that in his own life he has made quite a few "mistakes", and has had to face up to some difficult circumstances. However, his interest has been fed and sustained by some of the beneficial changes his trainees have experienced, even those surpassing his own!

During the last few years he has been able to redesign and largely revise his insights and understandings about the nature and influence of beliefs and how to create reality with them. This book is the result of those endeavours.

ABOUT THE SPONSOR

Martin McLeod, 60, is a chartered surveyor and has been married to Shelby for 35 years. They have four children and five grandchildren. Martin has led what he believes to have been a very happy, successful and fulfilling life.

Martin identifies himself with the theme and scope of this book, recognising that it contains in general terms the principles upon which he has progressed his own life.

Having embarked on this project with Julian, Martin introduced his son John, 26, whose artistic and spiritual nature led him to contribute to the symbolic ideas inherent in the illustrations. In 1996, John went through a period of accelerated spiritual growth, including a detailed study of Buddhism. Martin stresses that the author has not suggested or recommended any belief system of any kind to readers.

On the strength of Martin's and John's faith and belief in Julian's project, they both participated in the inspiration and support, including the finance and editorial suggestions, to bring this book to publication.

ABOUT THE PUBLISHING EDITOR

Fil Madden graduated in 1974 and has led a career in publishing both as a freelance and an employee. A life-long seeker of the central truths (if any), he has explored many philosophies and paths, and has undertaken deep personal work and some shamanic training. He is a student of writing and music.

He says: "It has taken me decades to fully realise that my outer life experiences and circumstances, especially the difficult ones, have reflected the landscape of my dream world. To change my outer I have had to work on the inner. To do otherwise is ultimately wasted effort.

It has been my experience, as well as my belief, that I always get what I ask for. I 'asked for' a project like this book to work on. It came, and has greatly improved the quality of my working life and circumstances."

HOW THIS BOOK CAME TO BE

The outer practicalities of this book all occurred within only a few months, though all the central participants had held a "project-in-potential" in the realm of thought and belief for some time previously.

Julian had been teaching courses, and had already published a short booklet. He had been looking for a way to present his extended ideas to the world, but had felt limited. Then he met Martin as a result of a so-called chance meeting in a Totnes bookshop, who kindly offered to sponsor a new book.

Fil had been looking for viable new projects. He and Julian had occasionally discussed other ideas that had come to nothing. Then, after Julian received Martin's offer of sponsorship, he offered his production-editorial expertise, which both Julian and Martin accepted.

One could say that it was all "meant to be" - a combination of circumstances originating in the realm of thought and belief that brought together the right people of related beliefs and vision.

This book blends the best and simplest of current belief theories with Julian's own experiences, presented in an easy and accessible way for any reader. What you read now is proof that the principles set out in this book actually work.

FOREWORD

"Life is what we make it."

"We get out of life what we put in."

"That which we sow, so shall we reap."

"There is a cause for every effect."

These truths are much more than just well-known sayings. They hold immense potential and power to create change for the better in this world. Yet it is unfortunate that they remain so little understood and unaccepted by both individuals and society at large.

The human mind and the consciousness it holds is one of nature's most powerful and mysterious creations. And most mysterious and extraordinary of all, our consciousness has the capacity for self-reflection. In our consciousness we are the aspect of the universe that operates on the mental plane.

Through our minds, we are nature observing itself: we are nature doing itself. We inhabit, experience and observe a universe that operates on the principles of cause-and-effect, where phenomena originate on the mental plane.

This means that we can use our minds to choose our reality; because once we understand the universal principles of cause-and-effect, we can exploit them. That's what this book is about.

We can take all this as either blessing or curse, but it does mean that we can choose whether our lives are difficult or easy, miserable or joyful, empty and dull, or active and fulfilled.

So if you have picked up this book because you're looking for some Big Answers, you have probably already been asking yourself the Big Questions: "why am I unhappy/ unfulfilled/ stony broke/lonely ...?"

Those answers lie, as always, within. You've probably already reasoned that if you can discover some causes for your disillusionments and dissatisfactions in life, you can begin to do something about them - to turn your life around. In other words, the search for quality in your life starts within yourself.

This book has been written to facilitate your journey towards understanding the principles of thought and belief, of taking self-responsibility for your past experiences and, most importantly, designing and choosing your future ones.

What you think, feel and believe has a massive impact on the outer circumstances of your life. This is the core message of this book; and once you understand that, you will have in your hands an immensely powerful tool for living well, and for making those essential changes in the core of your being that create the life experiences and circumstances you've always wanted.

Some of the qualities of the human mind are elusive and "soft" - concepts such as imagination and intuition. Others, such as evidence and logic, we might call scientific and "hard". In your journey through these pages - through your thoughts and beliefs - you'll come across lots of such concepts. But don't worry if you feel you're neither intuitive nor scientific, mystic nor hard-headed. None of that matters - this book is for anyone.

It is intended to be friendly and easy to use. It doesn't preach or instruct, it lays down no rules or regulations, and forces no beliefs or viewpoints on you. If you're looking to be told what to do, you'll be disappointed.

It is structured and logical, with a clear progression. Used well, it is your guide to help you improve the quality of your life: to help you gain the experiences you want, to help you achieve whatever you've always wanted to achieve, to help you enter the environment you've always wanted ... to help you pursue joy, success, happiness and fulfilment.

We want you to succeed, and we wish you every happiness and success in whatever you choose to believe and do in the future.

Above all, believe in yourself!

Martin W McLeod FRICS (chartered surveyor)

ACKNOWLEDGMENTS

I would like to thank Toni and Lee Preisler, Leonard Orr, Sondra Ray, Dom, Robert Fritz, M.M.Y., Douglas Cockbain, Roger Joesbury, Leslie, Saskia and Daisey for all their ideas, assistance and inspiration.

A special thanks goes to Martin and John McLeod for believing in me and this project, and to Fil Madden for all the editing and production assistance.

Julian Tytherleigh, Totnes, South Devon
April 1997

INTRODUCTION

This book is a simple and straightforward **introductory guide** to the theory and reality of beliefs and experience. It is intended for the general reader and, unlike some other books available, does not contain beliefs or views that you have to accept. Instead, it provides a framework to consider, question and explore and decide upon the nature and contents of your own beliefs. It could be said that there are too many experts writing on too many subjects; but here, you are encouraged to be your own expert in the field that only you know best: your own life and the experiences you have, or want to have.

The style of the book is deliberate and may prove to be controversial to the sceptical reader. But it has been designed as a theoretical approach from which to examine, explore and discover important belief structures. It is all open to question! The exercises, text and insights provided are to promote a hands-on way to assist you to establish a clearer understanding of your own views and beliefs, no matter what they are.

The emphasis is on managing, evolving and, if necessary, changing beliefs in the context of understanding and knowing the relationship between beliefs and what is experienced. How else do we create what we experience?

This book is

 a view of the theory, logic, structure and mechanics of beliefs

 an evaluation of the nature and effects of various kinds of belief

 about beliefs, creating, and experiencing.

This book is not

 about psychology, philosophy, religion, spirituality, therapy, the New Age, or anything "alternative"

 specific advice on what to think or how to lead your life.

I would like to encourage every reader to consider carefully the belief materials presented, and to slowly and methodically complete all the exercises. Also, I apologise for having to use the interchangeable terms "you", "they", and "a person" - I just want to be clear and relaxed about style.

I know that with the ability to find, discreate old beliefs and create new beliefs, you can have the ability to manage and direct your life more successfully; and thereby live in greater harmony with what you love and value most in your life and in your heart. Personal happiness and quality life experiences can follow from this. Personal belief integration and awareness can lead to wholeness of being and an increased ability to live more deliberately as one truly desires.

Sometimes life experiences and events just happen without any proper reason or explanation, and often we get results and effects we don't expect. As in science, like all areas of knowledge and understanding, experiences and facts can often be dismissed or disbelieved to protect much-cherished views and beliefs. What was once believed may now prove to be uncertain - meaning that old beliefs become open to change. Perhaps that is the way it has always been in the world and in our lives!

I hope this book provides some illumination and assistance for those seeking insight and change. Nevertheless, it is up to you, the reader, to decide for yourself what you want to believe and experience.

My best wishes ...

Julian Tytherleigh, Totnes, South Devon, April 1997

USING THIS BOOK

The exercises that occur throughout often suggest that you write something down in a private journal, which is where you can record all your responses.

 You will see this symbol to remind you not to make short-cuts and skip the writing-down stages! If you don't write things down, you won't get the full intended benefit of the exercise.

So to use this book fully, some kind of personal journal for note-taking and reflection is essential. It will be yours alone - no one else will see it unless you want them to. Some kind of high-quality large-format notebook with hard covers would be ideal. Some people like plain paper; others prefer lined. You can choose whatever kind you like.

One major advantage of having a loose-leaf journal is that you can make additions by inserting more pages in particular places. This means that you can put things in that may occur to you after you've done the exercises.

Also, if something occurs to you in connection with an exercise in, say, Chapter 1.2 and you're working on Chapter 6.4, then by all means go back. Covering old ground is almost never a waste of time, because that's one way that insight and understanding can develop.

It is also a good idea always to put the date on your work for future reference. Your journal will form a continuing record of your progress, and in later times you may read back with great interest to see how far you've come.

The material is structured logically. You'll probably do best to work through sequentially from beginning to end; though it's not meant to be read through quickly like a novel. Take your time - there's lots of material to absorb; and you'll benefit most by letting it sink in slowly.

HEADINGS

Throughout, you'll find these symbols:

 CONSIDER - a question or point of interest for you to think about

 IN SUMMARY - a review or general consideration

 EVIDENCE - specific proof that supports and verifies examples and viewpoints

 KEY INSIGHT - fundamental concepts to understand

 EXAMPLE - an illustration to a viewpoint or an insight

 NOTE - important ideas and concepts

 EXERCISE FOR YOU TO DO - something to do - for example, a contemplation exercise, and/or something to write down; you will also occasionally come across exercises that you can do with the assistance of a friend, partner or counsellor

 VIEWPOINT - a point of view created by the author

USE AND DEFINITIONS

Certain words are used throughout to mean particular things:

A BELIEF - the mental act, condition or habit of placing trust, faith or confidence in a person or thing; mental acceptance or conviction in the truth or existence of something, or a concept or group of concepts accepted by any group of people

TO CREATE - to cause to exist, bring into being, originate; to make or produce, to give rise to, to bring about

AN EXPERIENCE - the apprehension of an object, thought or emotion through the senses or mind

TO EXPERIENCE - to have active participation in events or activities, leading to the accumulation of knowledge or skill

TO INDOCTRINATE - to teach to accept a system of thought or belief

MANIPULATION - shrewd or devious efforts to manage or influence another person for one's own purposes

MIND - consciousness manifested in thought, perception, feeling, will, memory or imagination; the collective total of conscious and subconscious processes; the brain and central nervous system can function separately

FAITH - having belief in something one has no evidence for

POWER - the ability or capacity to act or perform in a certain way, to shape reality

REALITY - that which exists objectively and is experienced in fact

TO BE RESPONSIBLE - acknowledging authorship or creation of one's thoughts, beliefs and experiences; being the source, explanation or cause of something

A THOUGHT - a product of thinking; an idea, opinion or judgement

WILL - the mental faculty on and by which one deliberately chooses or decides on a course of action or endeavour

SECTION 1
ESSENTIAL CONCEPTS

1.1 THOUGHTS AND BELIEFS
1.2 HAVING THE POWER TO CREATE, OR NOT?
1.3 BEING SOURCE AND CREATING YOUR EXPERIENCES
1.4 FOCUS AND ATTENTION

"Man is what he believes."

Anton Chekhov (1861 - 1904)
Russian playwright.

"A man's life is what his thoughts make of it."

Ralph Waldo Emerson (1803 - 1882)
American poet, essayist and philosopher, whose works are regarded as a milestone in the development of American thought and literary expression.

"I think, therefore I am."

René Descartes (1596 - 1650)
French mathematician and philosopher who rejected all his previously held beliefs and asserted this notion as an inarguable truth.

*I can create the
experiences of
the world
I want.*

CHAPTER 1.1

THOUGHTS AND BELIEFS

Have you ever experienced one of those unusual coincidences - one of those inexplicable happenings that occur in life - and you are stuck for an adequate explanation as to why or how it happened? Many people have.

Have you ever had a specific clear thought, feeling or image in your mind about a person you know, or someone you want to contact? And then suddenly, out of the blue the telephone rings, or you walk around the next corner - and there they are! Have you ever said to them something like ...

"Ah, you won't believe this, but I was just thinking about you ..."

So how can you explain how these kinds of events occur, when you have actually had the thoughts **before** you had the event?

What explanation can there be to understand such happenings? The random statistical probability of this sort of event happening by chance is **very** low. But, no matter what the mathematics of probability are, if you yourself have experienced it you can surely be forgiven for suggesting that there could be a direct two-way link between our thoughts and feelings, and what actually happens in our lives.

Many writers, philosophers, psychologists, medical specialists and enlightened spiritual masters and teachers have suggested that there is such a real and direct link between our thoughts and beliefs, and the outer actualities.

One of the bases, or cornerstones, of Western philosophy is the well-known statement by René Descartes:

"I think, therefore I am."

It's not a particularly usable statement to the modern mind, nor is it a complete philosophy; otherwise it would be hypothetically possible to just change and direct your thoughts and - hey presto! - you have a new life just the way you want it!

But obviously, if it is true that thoughts affect our lives, there is great value in positive thinking. Yet the real power of the human mind comes from beliefs that are held as valid and true to each individual, and these are structured as belief patterns stored by the mind. These beliefs have significantly higher creative power and strength than just the constant stream of uncontrolled fleeting thoughts travelling through the mind each day. Thoughts can flow through the mind, but beliefs remain.

There is a fundamental difference between thought and belief. This explains how many people have set out with good thoughts and intentions to change their lives - but after some initial and encouraging results have returned, discouraged and disappointed, to a similar situation or set of circumstances from which they originally wanted to escape.

Such failure is probably because they did not also change their **core**, or **key**, beliefs, which form the underlying invisible building-blocks in their life. Without changing these there is a tendency to just drift back to where they were before, or to expend vast quantities of time and effort accomplishing only minor changes.

A thought is like a tiny molecule or brainwave particle that is generated in the mind. A belief, on the other hand, is a particular thought sequence or pattern of meaning that the mind holds **constantly** (or believes in) to be valid or true to itself. The content and quality of both thoughts and beliefs can be composed of absolutely **anything**.

Beliefs can shape a person's life. Beliefs can also provide the basic mental structures and environment from which certain kinds of spontaneous or created thoughts can arise. Many readers may be confused with the currently popular term "creative thinking", which is quite different from the wider view this book advocates: that **all** human thought and belief has a direct effect on, and relationship to, the quality, content, events, circumstances, experiences and direction of people's lives. It even creates our perceptions, our language, and even, collectively, the world we live in.

Let's look again at the difference between a person's thoughts and their beliefs. It's easy to be fairly aware of the thoughts we have. But many of the important beliefs a person holds are usually invisible; that is, held just out of everyday awake perceptions, at a level below normal conscious functioning and behaviour. This collection of "invisible" beliefs has a powerful impact on a person's life; and many of the chapters and activities that follow are designed to allow you to search for, discover and change your hidden beliefs.

 KEY INSIGHTS

★   There is a difference between thought and belief.

★   Your most important beliefs are those that
     are held with feelings.

In everyday language, the word "belief" is usually associated with either political, religious or other personal views held by someone. But beliefs also influence and cover the full and complete aspects of a person's life, including, for example, beliefs about

Oneself

Living today

Work and money

Relationships and other people

Love

Health

How outside influences affect you

The meaning and purpose of life

... and about absolutely everything else!

In fact, the totality of a person's life is dominated by the existence and creation of thoughts and beliefs. Thoughts and beliefs form the invisible connections between someone's inner state and their external reality. It's there, too, that the power resides that enables any person to live well, or poorly, in this world. Unfortunately, the reality for many people is that life is hard.

Modern science still has no complete understanding of how the human mind and brain work - but any casual observer can see that it does. The human mind routinely demonstrates tremendous agility, depth and power, and routinely applies itself to create so many wonderful things.

★   Most people would say they think there is a possible relationship between what a person thinks and believes, and what happens in their life ...

☆   some would say that there is a definite relationship ...

★   and a few believe that there is a direct and actual **cause-and-effect** relationship between them.

So what evidence is there to support the truth of this third viewpoint?

 EVIDENCE

Look around and observe the many everyday objects that people own and use in their lives - cars, houses, computers, books, money and electrical appliances.

Where did all of these **originate** from?

Answer: they were all thought up, created, and designed, in someone's mind first, before they were made for real.

The human mind creates things with thoughts - and any argument that tries to disprove this assertion must use thought to try and do so!

KEY INSIGHT

★ People create things with their thoughts. Thoughts can be entertained, modified or acted upon. Any thought, concept or idea constantly held in the mind (or believed in) becomes a belief.

EXAMPLE

Here's a simple story to explain how people create their experiences with thoughts, beliefs and actions:

Everyone knows how to make a cup of tea. It's a straightforward activity incorporating a few simple actions performed in a particular sequence. It all starts with a thought or desire "I'd like some tea", which focuses the mind, directs the body to act in a certain way to produce the desired result - the tea.

Here are the basic elements of this everyday creative thought / belief/ action/result cycle:

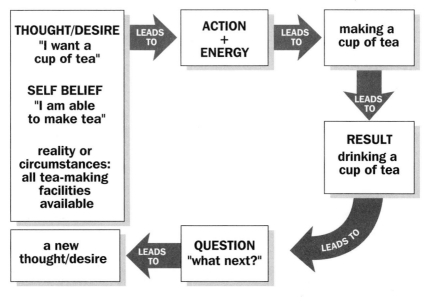

The same components can be used to design, create and experience anything at all, up to and including, no less than the overall direction, content and quality of a person's life. But some people don't **believe** that that is possible, or that they can do this by using the same principles as making tea!

The one key component usually overlooked by them in this creative cycle is the **beliefs** in their mind, which can either allow them or deny them the possibility of creating their preferred overall lifestyle.

The central theme of this book is for you to be able to explore the crucial role that beliefs can play in determining the quality of your everyday life. Some religions describe the power of belief as "karma", meaning that there are consequences to a person's thoughts, beliefs and actions: they experience the results of what they believe. Some call this spiritual law; others say it is simply the power of belief. But really, it is just **cause** and **effect**.

 EXERCISE FOR YOU TO DO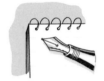

> Start to make some notes
> in your journal.

Do you believe there is a cause-and-effect relationship to some of the things you experience in your life?

What do you believe about this?

What evidence or experiences can you think of that support what you believe?

 EVIDENCE

Observe the natural world around you. Can you see that for every **effect** there is some kind of **cause** responsible?

> Jot down some examples.

KEY INSIGHTS

★ **For every effect there is a cause.**

☆ Sometimes the cause may be unknown, but there is always a cause.

☆ **Therefore, it is logical to suggest that for every effect (experience, event or creation) you have in your life, there is some cause responsible for it.**

So if thoughts, beliefs and actions are contributing causes that create the effects and results people experience, why do so many people seem to have major problems with their lives, being unable to effectively improve the quality of daily life?

 KEY INSIGHT

★ People can change their thoughts and actions easily enough, but the beliefs that have the real power that govern their lives, which are often held deep in their mind, are usually out of their everyday awareness, and are not necessarily easily found, accessed or changed.

Here are some other reasons why people find it difficult to create the quality of experiences they want and the kind of life they desire:

1   Some people have contradictory, unhelpful, limited or negative beliefs.

2   Some people find it easier to blame someone or something else for what they are experiencing, rather than claim the power and authorship of creating their own lives.

3   Some people have complicated and entrenched layer upon layer of belief patterns that make it more difficult for them to create the kind of life they want. Sometimes this enables people to distort or

misrepresent the objective facts and the truth about their life.

4   Some people genuinely believe they do not have the power, right or
      ability to change their lives - and so the power of belief ensures that
      their frame of mind becomes a reality - so providing the reflection
      and evidence of their belief.

5   There is an actual difference between what people say, think, pretend,
      or **want** to believe - and what they actually **do** believe!

6   Beliefs conditioned and indoctrinated into people from parents,
      society and other cultural sources can diminish their ability to believe
      and create the life experiences they want.

7   There are religious, political and financial groups of people in the
      world with an interest in keeping people away from their own
      power, independence, and freedom of choice.

   Modern science has only recently begun to understand the incredible
magic of the human mind. The exact power and influence of human
thoughts and belief has been very underestimated. Modern science is
forced to hold a viewpoint of scepticism towards the notion that belief has
any demonstrable effect in the external world: thought and belief are
invisible, undefinable, elusive and therefore unquantifiable for scientific
evaluation and study ... even though they actually exist.

   It isn't possible to try and estimate the nature and creative power of
thought and belief in the human mind. But there are many examples of
incredible human endeavours, and accounts of quite extraordinary events
that happen to people, and these have added huge weight to the
hypothesis of the power of belief. So whatever the inabilities of empirical
science to prove or disprove, we can definitely say that the beliefs held by
a person can hugely influence the creation and quality of their life.

   Many professionals and specialists in the fields of medicine, therapy,
business, training and sports coaching agree that a person's overall state
of mind (and set of beliefs they live by and operate through) can directly

influence their performance and the quality of their learning and achievement. In some instances, it may not just be a case of "mind over matter" but rather, as someone like Uri Geller can demonstrate, "mind **with** matter".

If the human mind is, at least in theory, unlimited in how it can be applied to shaping life experiences, then likewise the power of thoughts and belief **must** also be unlimited. The problem for science is tantalising: how would an empirical scientist devise an experiment to prove or disprove the notion that the key to human existence lies in the power of thought and belief? Besides the preconceived belief prejudices of the scientific experimenter, how could one use the very same apparatus and subject matter to test its own validity?

 VIEWPOINTS

1   Beliefs influence **all** aspects of life.

2   You and your beliefs function together, interacting in sets or collections of associated beliefs.

3   Beliefs create your experiences. So to discover and locate the exact nature of your most important and influential beliefs, look inside yourself and into the quality, content and shape of the real experiences, events and circumstances you have in your life. Experiences mirror beliefs.

4   Beliefs are also the filters and lenses through which we perceive and interpret the world.

5   Your deepest truest feelings are contained in, and created from, some of your most important beliefs.

 IN SUMMARY

All your thoughts, beliefs and actions have a direct and powerful effect upon your body, your life and your life experiences.

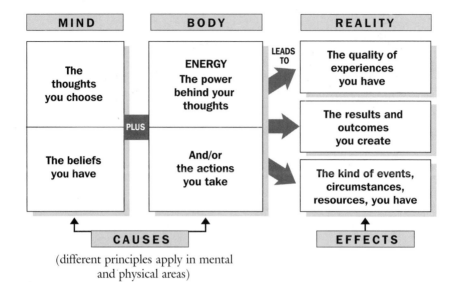

MIND	BODY	REALITY
The thoughts you choose	ENERGY The power behind your thoughts	**LEADS TO** The quality of experiences you have
PLUS		The results and outcomes you create
The beliefs you have	And/or the actions you take	The kind of events, circumstances, resources, you have

CAUSES   **EFFECTS**

(different principles apply in mental and physical areas)

KEY INSIGHT

☆ It is not just the range and quality of beliefs a person may hold, but the ones they choose to act on the most, that become the most significant.

EXERCISE FOR YOU TO DO

Make a list of some of the things you believe in.

Now consider whether what you experience in your life is consistent with, or relates to, any of the beliefs you have written down.

All effects must have causes. So in order to deliberately alter the effects, one needs to change the original causes that are responsible, if those causes lie within one's sphere of control.

The mind and body function under different principles of operation: almost all physical movement requires the expenditure of energy and effort, whereas the mind usually works best in a relaxed (non-stressed) effortless state.

NOTE

Physical bodily movement requires effort and energy.

Mental flexibility and change happens most easily with effortlessness, as mental struggle and overeffort are normally self-defeating.

Therefore, different operating principles apply in the physical and mental realms of human experience.

 EXERCISE FOR YOU TO DO

Exercise aim: to demonstrate the power of the mind and its influence over the functioning of the body.

What to do

1   Enlist the help of a willing friend for a few minutes.

2   Ask them to stand upright and follow this procedure.

3   Extend their dominant arm and ask them to close their eyes.

4   Get them to visualise in the mind a beam of light or bar of metal running through the arm, and tell them what you are about to do to it, so they know.

5   Say "hold" and ...

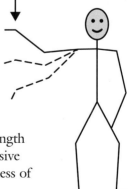

... push downwards firmly, but not forcefully, on the arm.

6   Notice the amount of resistance and strength the arm has. You don't need to use excessive or sudden force - gentle, sustained firmness of pressure is adequate.

7   Stop, and ask them to open the eyes.

8   Repeat the same procedure, but this time, as a comparison, get your friend to visualise a negative or distressing event they have experienced sometime in their life. While they hold this picture in their mind, test the arm again in exactly the same manner.

9   Notice: is there any significant difference in arm strength and its ability to resist your downward pressure? Observe what happens.

Expected results

Nearly everyone, if using an open and relaxed state of mind and not using excessive amounts of willpower to thwart or deliberately disprove this exercise, will respond in the following way.

EXERCISE 1	EXERCISE 2

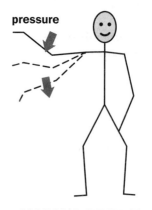

NORMAL RESULT:
a firm arm

NORMAL RESULT:
the arm is much weaker and cannot resist the same amount of pressure; therefore it drops downwards

IN SUMMARY

You can try this simple experiment with anyone, anywhere. It demonstrates the power and influence of specific visual images held in the mind upon the functioning and efficiency of the body. Some thought concepts focus your energy, and others can disperse it!

EXERCISE FOR YOU TO DO

Exercise aim: to demonstrate the power of negative suggestion and thought on the mind.

What to do

1   Get the help of some people for a few minutes. Ask them to sit down and close their eyes.

2   Tell them this is a very simple mental exercise, but give no other details.

3   Say that you are going to instruct them to follow a simple command.

4   Instruct them that they absolutely must **not** see a green hippopotamus!

5   Allow ten seconds to pass.

6   Ask them to open their eyes and tell you what they saw.

Expected result

Most people will see something green and hippopotamus-like. A few, with very good mental discipline, won't.

 EVIDENCE

Try it and see what happens!

IN SUMMARY

The mind can be very easily influenced by the power of negative suggestion.

Therefore:

1   What you try and avoid happening in your life (or seeing as an outcome in your mind) something you don't want to happen - by the power of negative suggestion - you give it power and credibility, thereby making it more likely to happen or be attracted to you!

2   Whatever you mentally fight against - you will tend to reinforce.

3   Whatever you focus on the most with your thoughts and beliefs will tend to influence your life the most!

4   The power of mental focus and repetition works for both positive **and** negative suggestion.

So, where does the energy and power come from which creates and empowers our thoughts?

From your life source, made from **pure awareness**. Any label, idea or belief placed upon this pure awareness must automatically become consciousness. With, through and because of consciousness, all things are created and experienced. Consciousness contains the fundamental elements of creation.

Much of this theory defies proper scientific explanation; but the subjective proof of it is that you **know** what you experience **is** real in your life - there can be no argument about that. The realness of the personal experience of being alive is the evidence we have that consciousness exists - it is as simple and irrefutable as that! You can't argue that your personal experiences are not real!

Scientists acknowledge that people know they are conscious - but no one really knows **what** consciousness itself is. Human beings have evolved a unique evolutionary survival mechanism by having consciousness, and notably the development of language and intellectual reason. We have also developed the ability to create new meanings, understandings, interpretations, and to be able to learn new things about ourselves and our world.

Of particular significance is the human ability to be self-aware, and to be able to use concepts such as the past, present and future in a manner that other species cannot do.

The essence of self-consciousness in humans is simply the ability to be consciously aware of what is happening to you, and it is not dependent on any other form of consciousness to do so. Although recent scientific researches suggest that the total human brain comprises at least 400 computer-like parts functioning interactively, there is no great understanding of what consciousness and awareness actually is, because the structure and biochemistry of the brain offers no explanation that completes our knowledge. This is the point at which we simply arrive at a view - that there is **no** great mystery to awareness and consciousness, just an acknowledgement that it is there, and that's what we experience our lives with and through! Understanding those concepts is not the same as experiencing them for real.

 EVIDENCE

You can **only** be reading this book **through** your own consciousness.

 CONSIDER

Without being conscious and aware, what would our lives be like?

 EXERCISE FOR YOU TO DO

Contemplate what exists in the space between your thoughts.

HAVING THE POWER TO CREATE, OR NOT?

The power and creation of our existence and experiences resides in our thoughts and beliefs. Thoughts and beliefs are similar to the software programming in computers. If you have the ability to choose and direct your thoughts and beliefs, you will be able to direct your life and, thereby, your future.

Without the ability to effectively manage beliefs, there can be no real choice, no real freedom, no power and no spiritual enlightenment. The quality of your life experiences is largely determined by the beliefs you carry, and your ability to change your beliefs, and thereby your experiences.

This chapter is probably one of the most fundamental in this book, because belief in your ability and power to create is more important than any theoretical understanding. Knowing what power is, is not the same as the real and actual experience of it.

However other people have defined the word "power", in this book it means:

"... the ability, authority and means to create one's life and one's experiences in line with one's own wishes."

 VIEWPOINT

Some people do not seem to have the ability to create for themselves the kinds of experiences and life they want.

 KEY INSIGHT

☆ The beliefs people hold and the actions they take with these beliefs determine the circumstances and the quality of their lives.

VIEWPOINTS

Why do some people seem to have little power and ability to successfully self-manage their beliefs and the quality of their lives?

Some possible explanations

1   Some people tend to deny or fear their own natural creative abilities and power.

2   Some people tend to underestimate what they can do and what they can achieve.

3   Some people are not necessarily aware of how self-imprisoning their present beliefs can be.

4   Some people make and believe other things or other people to be more powerful or influential than themselves in determining their life.

5   Some people have collected an array of social, educational and cultural beliefs that often confuse and mislead them, thereby extinguishing their ability to create and experience their own freely chosen beliefs.

6   Some people keep themselves too busy and overstressed with the on-going commitments of their lives, so that they don't even have time to consider, let alone create, the life they really want to lead.

7   Some people have already become discouraged and disappointed by past failures in trying to change or improve their lives. They have learned that trying to change what their realities are, without also altering their key or core beliefs, tends to lead them back into experiencing similar circumstances or to repeat patterns of behaviour. Real, lasting and fundamental change can be elusive without proper and relevant belief alteration or management.

8   Some people have beliefs that render themselves powerless, or they

open themselves to becoming victims of unwanted accidents, events, circumstances or other people's wishes or actions. Indoctrinated beliefs are often unseen by those forced to wear them.

9   Some beliefs, due to their nature and content, are easier than others to build your life with.

KEY INSIGHTS

☆ Quality thoughts and beliefs lead to quality life experiences!

☆ Most persistent or personal problems are either created or influenced by beliefs containing some form of powerlessness.

☆ The reality caused by the use of power in society is the existence of either domination or submission between individuals or groups of people. However, power can be shared!

EXERCISE FOR YOU TO DO

Jot down all the situations you face in your life now in which you perceive you are powerless to influence or change easily. Find at least ten.

PERCEPTIONS OF POWER AND RESPONSIBILITY - A BELIEF PERSPECTIVE

The power to change and create your life a particular way is influenced by the amount of responsibility you extend to each situation. Power and responsibility go together; it is only possible to change or create what you can be directly or somehow responsible for.

If you don't believe you have any power or influence over creating a situation you have experienced, why expect and assume you automatically have the ability to alter it? It is a form of belief powerlessness to perceive that any situation you experience can influence you more than you can influence it.

NOTE

Being responsible means that you can claim authorship of your experiences. This includes all experiences you cause **directly** through your actions, and all experiences you experience and cause to create **indirectly** through your beliefs. Being responsible also implies having enough awareness to acknowledge that you create your experiences. Responsibility is about owning up to being the cause of situations, rather than administering blame.

RESPONSIBILITY - A BELIEF PERSPECTIVE

In order to examine and understand the beliefs, and the experiences caused by them, what follows now is the theoretical framework that forms the key component of this book. It is up to you to decide how much, if any, of this you accept and believe, as some might say it is controversial. But it should provide a reflection of what you truly believe about these things.

People are responsible for their actions

and therefore it follows that ...

People are responsible for what they choose to think and believe

and therefore it follows that ...

People are responsible for what they experience

and therefore it follows that ...

**People are responsible for what is done
to them either by the beliefs they hold that
allow certain things to happen, or by the lack
of adequate belief to prevent things
from happening**

and therefore it follows that ...

**People are responsible for their own lives and
all aspects of what they create and experience.
Therefore your reality reflects what you believe.**

SHARED EXPERIENCES

A person may also be responsible for experiencing with or what someone else was initially responsible for creating. Many experiences and creations are joint or shared, sometimes by a few or by many people.

FORMS OF DISEMPOWERMENT

If you place or put the cause or source of creation of any situation you experience outside of yourself by disowning or denying authorship, or by blaming other people or other things other than yourself for your experiences, you are using your thoughts and beliefs to effectively disempower yourself. It is much easier for people to blame and accuse than to admit, but the courage of owning authorship of your own personal experiences can directly lead to the rediscovery of the real and fundamental beliefs that create your life.

 EXERCISE FOR YOU TO DO

Here are some questions to consider:

Do you believe you are responsible for your actions?

Do you believe you are responsible for what you choose to think **and** believe?

Do you believe you are responsible for what you experience?

Do you believe you are responsible for what is directly and indirectly done to you?

Do you believe you are completely responsible for your own life and **some, most or all** aspects of what you experience?

If you do not believe you are completely responsible for creating **all** your experiences and your own life, **who or what holds the power and influence** (and the responsibility) for the way your life now is?

So what beliefs do you hold about these things?

GUIDES TO INCREASING PERSONAL POWER

These points are clarified in later chapters; but for now, here's a summary.

1   Acknowledge personal authorship and responsibility for all your thoughts, beliefs, actions and experiences.

2   Discover your key or core beliefs - what you truly believe.

3   Switch off or discreate all unhelpful, outdated and self-sabotaging beliefs.

4   Create new beliefs that support your quality of being.

5   Choose specific goals you want, and then take action. Determine your present and future.

6   Align your beliefs to assist making your goals happen easily.

7   Believe you have the power and ability to achieve real improvements in the quality of your living circumstances.

8   Do what serves your best self-interests, and enjoy your life. After all, it is not selfish to assert the right to lead your own life.

9   Listen to your feelings, follow your intuition and accept and appreciate how life unfolds and evolves for you.

 EXERCISE FOR YOU TO DO

Take five minutes to be alone. Sit down, relax and be quiet, and close your eyes. Imagine you have unlimited power to change or create your life in any way you desire. Contemplate what this feels like ...

After some time, open your eyes and consider your feelings. Jot them down.

THE POWER AND LOCATION OF BELIEFS

So how does the power of beliefs create what you experience as reality? Beliefs function and are stored in the subconscious mind, below normal conscious levels of mental activity and underneath everyday awareness. Consider, for example, how you acquired the learnt skills of being able to cook, to speak a foreign language, or to drive a car. Everyone has done at least some of these things.

Take learning to drive. Like the other examples, at first everything was unfamiliar and new and, for each manoeuvre or sequence, you consciously thought yourself through each step. After a while, and some experience, you learned the skill and how to perform sequential tasks automatically. Your mind stored all the information and experience needed to learn, **and** the relevant skill, at below the conscious level, where it remains.

So, every time you use a skill, or any language or information, your mind accesses it and makes it readily available to you from the subconscious mind. **It is the same for all your beliefs.**

You may wonder about the success secrets of the rich and powerful, but it's no mystery. Their crucial and determining beliefs might seem invisible, but it's only because they have trained themselves to use their positive beliefs, which operate automatically and underneath their usual focus of awareness. That's why, looking from the outside at least, things appear effortless to them.

KEY INSIGHTS

☆   A person can have any number of beliefs, of any nature, arranged in any order of importance.

★   Your beliefs are stored in your subconscious mind.

☆   It is not just **what** a person believes that matters, but **how** they believe it.

★   A person's beliefs tend to affect each other and affect how they function together.

☆   The number, nature, structure and arrangement of a person's beliefs will determine what they create and what they experience.

★   The belief systems at the core of our being create the energy centres (or chakras) which govern our bodies and our lives. These chakras hold patterns of consciousness; therefore, whoever sees the world in terms of love and compassion will create that reality with their belief system.

EXAMPLES

This diagram represents a collection of associated and interrelated beliefs. Belief no. 3 has more power and influence to create, as the others help justify and support its existence.

A collection or set of beliefs containing a dominant belief

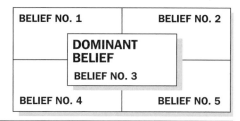

A RECTANGLE LIKE THIS REPRESENTS A BELIEF		
BELIEF NO. 1		BELIEF NO. 2
	DOMINANT BELIEF	
	BELIEF NO. 3	
BELIEF NO. 4		BELIEF NO. 5

A person holding a collection of related and mutually assisting beliefs is more likely to be able to change or move their life easily in a specific desired direction; because the **alignment** and **relationship** of beliefs to each other can determine their influence and effectiveness.

AN ALIGNED SET OF BELIEFS

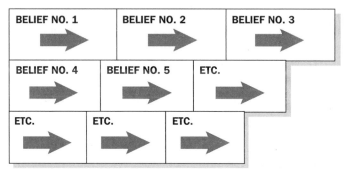

Now compare this with:

AN UNALIGNED SET OF BELIEFS

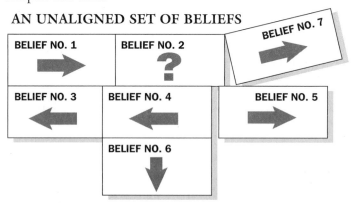

A person holding a conflicting set of beliefs out of alignment **and** disassociated from each other is more likely to experience some of these consequences:

★   having no clear direction

☆   feeling confused or unsure about what they really want
     next in their life

★ achieving few lasting or meaningful results or personal achievements of merit

☆ often experiencing feelings of frustration, and feeling limited and weighed down by too many demands on their time and energy

★ frequently experiencing a loss of energy, drive, purpose and enthusiasm for anything.

 KEY INSIGHT

☆ The arrangement or alignment of any individual or set of beliefs is as important as the nature of those beliefs. For every belief can affect the role of any other belief.

 EXERCISE FOR YOU TO DO

Consider this question:

Have you ever had, over a period of years, the reoccurring experience of consistently missing some of your desired goals?

Describe some examples that come to mind.

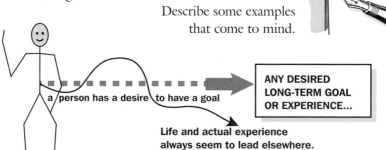

 KEY INSIGHT

☆ The kinds of beliefs a person holds may **not** lead them in the direction of achieving goals or desires, but away from them!

VIEWPOINTS

☆   Examine and change, if necessary, beliefs that affect the achievement of specific goals.

★   Realign your beliefs to specific goals.

☆   Clearing unhelpful beliefs increases your personal ability to create.

★   The greater number of beliefs you hold, the more difficult it can be to create through them.

☆   The lesser number of beliefs you hold, the easier it can be to create through them.

★   Creating something is easier without limiting, negative or contradictory beliefs.

☆   By unravelling and realigning your core beliefs, you can more easily know and create what you most value in your heart!

★   In discovering your true beliefs, you have to allow the factual evidence of reality and the testament of experience to reflect back what you really believe.

 KEY INSIGHT

☆   Without fundamental belief change, any effort used to change your life may not be successful or long-lasting. When your key beliefs remain unchanged, you are likely to experience a return to similar circumstances, or to have repetitive life-experience patterns.

 EXERCISE FOR YOU TO DO

Here's a question:

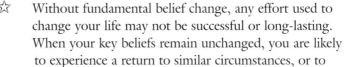
Have you ever tried to change your life in a significant manner, only to find yourself, sometime later, back in the familiar situation like the one you were trying to change?   Jot down some examples.

BEING SOURCE AND CREATING YOUR EXPERIENCES

*"The game of life is not so much in holding a
good hand as playing a poor hand well."*

H T Leslie

If you find, like most people, that deciding what you really want is a
problem, look to your **conscious aware will**. It is there that your real
powers of decision, determination, choice and discrimination reside.

EXERCISE FOR YOU TO DO

Exercise aim: to demonstrate the effect the **will** can have on a
person's mind by deliberately deciding on an action.

What to do

Deliberately choose to smile - until you feel happy or joyful.

EXERCISE FOR YOU TO DO

Exercise aim: to demonstrate the effect the **will** can have on a
person's physical action by deliberately deciding on holding a
deliberate state of mind.

What to do

Choose to think to yourself "I am happy", and keep going
until you start smiling!

KEY INSIGHTS

☆ You **are** aware will (see meanings, page xv).

★ Your will rules all - it can determine belief creation and
viewpoint.

☆   Your mind can influence your body (and emotions) and your body
can influence your mind.

 NOTE

☆   You create your experiences through your
beliefs, but determine what you can achieve and do
through your **will**.

If we take it that someone is responsible for the experiences they have
in their life, it therefore follows that a person is either

☆   a prisoner of their own beliefs, or

★   the master of them and able to direct and manage
their life effectively.

The first category defines disempowerment, and the second is the
basis of personal empowerment. The difference is purely whether a
person consciously uses their thoughts, beliefs and actions in a deliberate
way to steer their life towards desired outcomes or experiences; or
whether they are constantly reacting or responding to a haphazard
stream of events that they do not seem able to control or direct, and that
don't serve their well-being.

Being the creative source in your own life is not just a theoretical or
intellectual notion, but an actual living experience of "knowing"
instinctively that you have the power and ability, sometimes only
realisable in small but gradually increasing steps, to determine your
experiences.

 NOTE

☆   Some people have lost their own natural ability to be the
source creator of their own life, simply because their
minds are overburdened by too many beliefs, and their lives are
dominated by too many considerations.

Behind all your thoughts and beliefs resides the energy and power of **pure awareness** that is your **life force and source**. This life source makes your thoughts and beliefs real. The only way you can know and experience anything is by holding beliefs that

★ define who you are

☆ enable you to perceive and interpret what you experience.

However, these self-defining beliefs, or self-beliefs, form the basis from which other beliefs function. All self-beliefs containing the definition of what **"I am"**, or what **"I am not"**, naturally possess great influence over our ability to create, as they determine our inherent qualities and state of being. This is why when **"I am..."** beliefs are aligned to **"I can..."** beliefs, people become empowered.

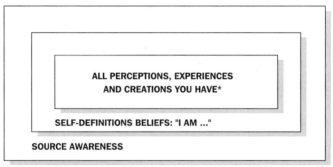

ALL PERCEPTIONS, EXPERIENCES
AND CREATIONS YOU HAVE*

SELF-DEFINITIONS BELIEFS: "I AM ..."

SOURCE AWARENESS

* You can only perceive or experience anything through self-defining beliefs. These same self-defining beliefs were originally created from source awareness (see Section 3, "Self-beliefs and identity").

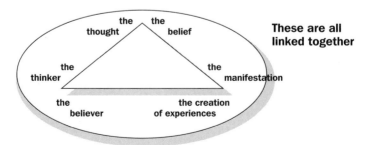

the thought

the belief

the thinker

the manifestation

the believer

the creation of experiences

These are all linked together

EXERCISE FOR YOU TO DO

Take some time out to contemplate

☆   whether you think that all of life on planet earth is somehow linked together

★   whether you think that all aspects of your life are somehow linked together.

 VIEWPOINT

We all have beliefs that define ourselves, what we have, what we do, where we are, etc. These beliefs define what is us, and what is not us. Our connection to all these aspects of life depends on what we define as being within ourselves or outside ourselves. As these fundamental beliefs influence our connection to the creation and experience of life, **any** viewpoints or perceptions of separation will automatically inhibit our ability to create or discreate.

 EXERCISE FOR YOU TO DO

This is about perception and separation.

Sit down and relax for a while - somewhere where you won't be disturbed.

First read through the questions below, then do the contemplation, and use your journal to jot down your responses afterwards.

Observe and contemplate a familiar object within your field of view. Allow your awareness to rest gently on this item for a few minutes.

1   Can you perceive the object as being different or separate from you?

2   What insights did you gain?

EXERCISE FOR YOU TO DO

This exercise is about releasing or surrendering judgements or labels you place on other people or situations in your life.

☆ Choose a person or situation you know about whom or about which you have a particular or negative viewpoint.

★ Relax, and mentally focus on suspending this view of them.

☆ Contemplate replacing this judgement or label with another new different one.

★ Can you perceive them differently now?

Write down what you experience and feel.

NOTES

Notice that any created or imposed perception, viewpoint or definition of **separateness** causes you to lose clarity, power or influence over whatever you are observing, because you are perceiving it as separate from you. Therefore, by reducing or eliminating the viewpoints or beliefs you hold that separate you from any creation or experience, you enhance being able to change or adapt these same creations or experiences.

Source awareness is your infinite Higher Self that exists without separation from anything. You are the creator of your thoughts and beliefs, but you are not them. By deliberately reducing or removing separation, you can assume fuller responsibility for what you are experiencing.

Many therapies or training programmes do not, unfortunately, provide either the ability to renew the experience of being connected to source awareness, or the ability to create new beliefs and goals. Revisiting past memories and traumas does not automatically enhance your ability to create new beliefs and experiences; instead, it rather diminishes it, because your focus tends to rest on what happened, rather than what you believed at the time.

 EXERCISE FOR YOU TO DO

1   Write down your current greatest fears.

Now consider each fear. What do you feel?

2   Write down your current greatest doubts.

Now consider each doubt. What do you feel?

CHAPTER 1.4
FOCUS AND ATTENTION

"We are what we repeatedly do. Excellence, then, is not an act, but a habit."   Aristotle

This chapter is about understanding how thoughts and beliefs create our lives through focus and attention.

Whatever thoughts and beliefs tend to fill our focus and attention on a regular and consistent basis naturally have more power than those that receive only fleeting attention.

NOTE

☆   The key to creating changes in your life is to change your mental viewpoint and to change **what** dominates your focus and attention.

EXERCISE FOR YOU TO DO

Sit down, close, your eyes, get comfortable, and relax. Take a couple of minutes to review mentally the events in your life over the past week.

Now consider **how** your attention lingers on certain things you deem important and **how** it resists considering other matters!

NOTE

★   When your attention is filled with **fixed** judgements (such as "this was good", "that was bad", etc) it tends to glue itself onto those actual experiences in your life that may be more stuck than other experiences.

☆   Repetitive thoughts and fixed attention make **any** type of creation (physical/material circumstances or emotional experiences) more solid, and tend to make those things more real and thereby draw them to you.

★ When attention is being used to create something, the mind can often become stuck on uncertainty. If it does, you can easily relieve it by directing your attention through the uncertainty directly onto the desired end result you want. Train your mind to just leave the uncertainty alone - drop it! Leapfrog over it! Keep focusing on the end result you want, even if there is no apparent way or means yet available for achieving it.

 EXERCISE FOR YOU TO DO

Exercise aim: to place and recall your focus from areas in your life where your attention is fixed.

Sit down, close your eyes, get comfortable, and relax. Focus upon something that you

☆ regularly focus your attention on, or

★ something you take very seriously or is personally sensitive to you.

Bring this matter into your mind, describe it in detail, and

☆ think of it in a light and humorous new way, or

★ expand it into an absolutely enormous problem, and then

☆ reduce it to a matter of minute importance.

Keep doing this until your fixed attention is released. Sometimes insights, solutions, relief from pain, releasing past traumas or emotional changes can be experienced by recovering your focus from a fixed area of attention.

Be prepared to do this exercise for long periods of time. Old traumas may resurface, but be persistent to see it through to its conclusion.

Expected result

With regular practice you will naturally develop the ability to shift your focus and attention freely, and to re-edit the way you think about things. This can help you in developing greater mental focus and attention on the things that matter to you. You can also reduce any tendency for your mind to divide its focus and concentration, so that the associated worries and confusions that often accompany this get smaller too. **This can lead to physical and emotional healings.**

 EXERCISE FOR YOU TO DO

Here's something simple to demonstrate the incredible power of your mind to manifest or create small objects, or the ability to attract certain items into your possession. It combines the power of thoughts and belief with the use of focus and deliberate attention.

Sit down, close your eyes, get comfortable, and relax.

1   Think of a small relatively inexpensive object of personal interest to you that you would like to possess - something that you could acquire if you set out to do so, but don't want to just go out and buy it for yourself.

2   Use your imagination for a couple of minutes to picture seeing this object for real, and being in your hands. Imagine its feel, colour, smell, size, and any other attributes or qualities you like. Focus on it being yours and the pleasure it gives you to own it.

3   Repeat this every day for two weeks and then observe whether this particular object comes into your life over the next two months.

 EXERCISE FOR YOU TO DO

Make some notes now.

1   On what or whom do you spend most of your time, attention and energy?

2   Is your time, attention and energy frequently scattered between many different things and people?

3   On **what** is your time, attention and energy focused the most?

4   What beliefs do you have about this situation?

5   Is this situation desired and wanted by you, or not?

IN SUMMARY

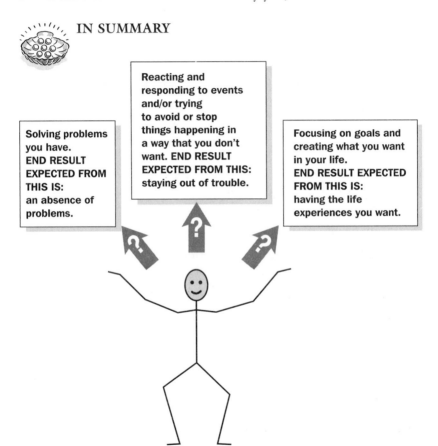

Solving problems you have. END RESULT EXPECTED FROM THIS IS: an absence of problems.

Reacting and responding to events and/or trying to avoid or stop things happening in a way that you don't want. END RESULT EXPECTED FROM THIS: staying out of trouble.

Focusing on goals and creating what you want in your life. END RESULT EXPECTED FROM THIS IS: having the life experiences you want.

WHAT DO YOU FOCUS UPON THE MOST?

SECTION 2
THE THEORY AND REALITY
OF BELIEF

2.1   A THEORY OF BELIEFS
2.2   A GUIDE TO DIFFERENT TYPES OF BELIEFS
2.3   HOW BELIEFS FUNCTION
2.4   BELIEF PATTERNS, STRUCTURES AND STRENGTH
2.5   BELIEF VARIABLES
2.6   PRESENT TIME, PAST AND FUTURE
2.7   THE EXPERIENCE OF REALITY
2.8   CREATING EXPERIENCES WITH BELIEFS
2.9   CHANGING BELIEFS

"Man is still the most extraordinary computer of all."

John F Kennedy (1917 - 1963)
President of the USA, 1961 - 1963.

*I can unravel
the jigsaw
puzzle of my
beliefs.*

A THEORY OF BELIEFS

*"Minds are like parachutes. They only function
when they are open."*   James Dewar

All the many different types of beliefs you have form together the basic
components of your life. These components are responsible for creating

★ THE EXPERIENCE OF WHO YOU ARE AND WHAT YOU ARE

☆ HOW YOU BEHAVE AND HOW YOU RESPOND TO
OTHER PEOPLE

★ HOW LIFE WORKS OR DOESN'T WORK FOR YOU

☆ WHAT YOUR LIFE DOES OR DOESN'T CONTAIN

★ WHAT HAPPENS IN YOUR LIFE AND THE DIRECTION
YOU CHOOSE

☆ THE CIRCUMSTANCES, CONDITIONS AND
OPPORTUNITIES THAT YOU HAVE.

 KEY INSIGHTS

★ BELIEFS CREATE YOUR OUTER REALITY.

☆ BELIEFS CAUSE EXPERIENCE.

★ BELIEFS PRECEDE (COME OR EXIST BEFORE) EXPERIENCE.

Therefore, it's correct to say that ...

☆ YOU CREATE YOUR EXPERIENCES ACCORDING TO WHAT
YOU BELIEVE

rather than ...

you create your beliefs from your experiences.

And ...

BELIEVING IS SEEING

rather than ...

seeing is believing.

After all ...

ONLY YOU KNOW WHAT YOU EXPERIENCE AND WHAT IS REAL FOR YOU.

Because ...

YOU AND YOUR EXPERIENCES ARE CONNECTED.

Reality is anything one believes it to be - made up of those things we believe to be **real**.

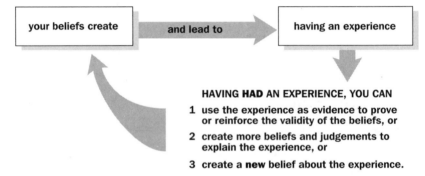

| your beliefs create | and lead to | having an experience |

HAVING HAD AN EXPERIENCE, YOU CAN

1 use the experience as evidence to prove or reinforce the validity of the beliefs, or

2 create more beliefs and judgements to explain the experience, or

3 create a **new** belief about the experience.

 **KEY INSIGHT**

★   To experience something as it truly is, is to be present with one's perceptions without expectation, judgement or definition.

To find the original creating beliefs, look **within** the nature of your experiences.

However ...

1   the original creating beliefs are often buried under lots of other additional beliefs and judgements

2   these beliefs are normally so familiar that the believer doesn't question them

3   these beliefs are usually simple and self-evident

4   these beliefs are usually held below a person's conscious level of everyday awareness.

So ...

You create, from source awareness, each successive moment of your existence: all your experiences including all your joys, sorrows, successes, failures, limitations and opportunities ... with the **total** collection of your beliefs.

 VIEWPOINT

The truth is not about **what** you or anyone created, but the fact that somehow you had some influence in creating it!

 KEY INSIGHT

☆   Truth is only relative to the point of view from which it is perceived ... because what you look **at**, and where you look **from**, determine your perception of what truth is.

 VIEWPOINT

Everyone's perception of what is true and believable is different.

 IN SUMMARY

All experienced realities are ultimately formed from beliefs.

A GUIDE TO
DIFFERENT TYPES OF BELIEF

Everyone has their own unique collection of opinions, thoughts and beliefs, and this collection changes and evolves continuously.

There seems to be an infinite variety of different beliefs that people hold to be true, and they are all valid or meaningful to those who create them.

This chapter is a simple guide to some of the differences between some broad categories or types of beliefs. **It's only a generalisation**, and it's not necessary for our purposes here to go too far with categorising.

Five types of belief are:

Type 1   emotionally appealing beliefs

Type 2   belief solutions and theories

Type 3   beliefs that depend on factual evidence

Type 4   intentionally created beliefs

Type 5   other kinds of beliefs.

KEY INSIGHT

★   Successful people, by which we mean those who are able to create the experiences and lives they actually want, tend to have many more beliefs in types 3 and 4 than in types 1 and 2.

TYPE 1   EMOTIONALLY APPEALING BELIEFS

Someone advocating a strongly emotional and appealing belief may use it to demand that another person should believe and act upon it. They can do this by making the belief recipient feel personally responsible for, or connected to, what is or is not happening.

Emotionally appealing beliefs can be used as a form of manipulation, a strategy to get someone to react or to take action in a manner in line with what the belief sender desires. Such beliefs are usually based on the emotions of fear, guilt, hatred, distrust or sympathy.

Examples

The planet is overpolluted - you must act to save it - NOW!

You are either part of the problem or part of the solution.

For every minute you don't act - someone will die.

If you don't buy this now, you'll miss out and be sorry!

When the day of judgement comes you'll burn in hell with all the other sinners!

This child is sick and needs your help today.

TYPE 2 BELIEF SOLUTIONS AND THEORIES

These kinds of beliefs are characterised by providing sensible and believable solutions and theories as to **"HOW IT IS"** or **"HOW THINGS ARE"** in your life and the real world.

Examples

You have to work hard to succeed at anything.

Every cloud has a silver lining.

You have to struggle to make a living.

It's all relative.

That's the way the cookie crumbles!

You have to learn from your mistakes.

Money doesn't grow on trees.

Look on the bright side - it wasn't meant to be.

You can't trust strangers.

I had no choice.

A change is as good as a rest.

TYPE 3 BELIEFS THAT DEPEND ON FACTUAL EVIDENCE

All these beliefs depend on factual and observable evidence to support their existence. The facts become so believable and incontrovertible that they become beliefs themselves.

Type 3 beliefs contain

1   the laws of science, all scientific testing, and scientific evidence (even though the so-called "laws of science" cannot prove that these laws exist!)

2   all technologies and the products of technology

3   all theoretical and academic knowledge

4   all religious philosophies, doctrines, creeds and moral ideas

5   all personal "facts" that are true and real in your life.

These are all objective beliefs based on

1   logical assumptions

2   evidence from the past

3   sensory experiences that people have had.

Examples

Space is infinite.

There is only one true religion.

Life evolves through evolution.

My computer works well.

You can't argue with the facts.

TYPE 4 INTENTIONALLY CREATED BELIEFS

These kinds of beliefs are specifically created by someone in order to acquire new perspectives and the playfulness of new experiences. It is believing deliberately for the desired purpose of experiencing. They are essential to being able to live deliberately in the manner you choose.

These type 4 beliefs are characterised by being self-created; therefore you can influence your experiences more flexibly, adaptively and influentially than you can with the other three types of belief.

TYPE 5 OTHER KINDS OF BELIEFS

There may be others but for now they are outside the scope of this book.

 KEY INSIGHT

☆   Deciding **what** you want to believe is the **fundamental** aspect of creating what you want in life.

 NOTE

Some people find it difficult to decide what to believe, because they have lived largely through and by either

★   indoctrinated or limited beliefs, or

☆   beliefs borrowed from other sources and other people

... and so they do not know how to create their own beliefs, nor how to use them.

Examples

There is always a simpler and easier way to do things.

Every experience I have teaches me a valuable lesson.

Life is fun!

I can do anything I set my mind to.

Whatever I do, everything works out perfectly for me.

I am safe and secure in this world.

I always make the right choices - I trust my intuition.

Other people appreciate knowing me.

I am open to adventure and love exploring new things in life.

... or whatever you want!

 EXERCISE FOR YOU TO DO

SELECT **ANY** BELIEF...
what kind of belief is it? (what is its nature?)

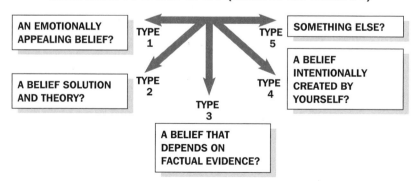

CONSIDER

Take a quiet 30 minutes alone somewhere to review and write down the beliefs you have. Consider what percentage, roughly, are self-created by you; and what remaining percentage have their origins from school, friends, family, the media, social, political and business organisations, and sources other than yourself.

Note: you can unconsciously "catch" beliefs from other people in a similar manner to the way some diseases are transmitted.

Use your private journal to jot down your insights.

CHAPTER 2.3

HOW BELIEFS FUNCTION

In the preceding chapters we looked at how the beliefs you hold in your subconscious have consequences in your life. Let's now consider a simple way to think about beliefs and how they work.

They radiate an energy field, or force field, rather like a magnet does, attracting experiences that are consistent to the belief. Over time, they tend to grow, get stronger, and become so familiar that they become unquestioned by the holder.

As most beliefs are stored and held below one's everyday level of conscious awareness, it is not always easy to see how beliefs

☆   collect evidence that supports the existence of a belief

★   filter out or disregard evidence that does not support the belief.

beliefs exclude and filter out experiences not consistent with themselves

EXPERIENCES REFLECT

BACK WHAT IS BELIEVED

A PERSON

BELIEFS RADIATE

OUTWARDS

thereby beliefs collect and attract evidence to support the continued proof and justification of themselves

KEY INSIGHT

☆   Personal reality (what is real) reflects what a person truly believes - which is not always the same as what they may be pretending or wanting to believe.

NOTES

★   **Any** belief has definition and dimension in consciousness.

☆   Believing (or having faith) is the conscious part of creating.

★   Believing creates the belief and then the experience.

KEY INSIGHT

☆   Existence is

BELIEVING*

INFLUENCES   AFFECTS

EXPERIENCING

* but the initial cause is always believing

And so ...

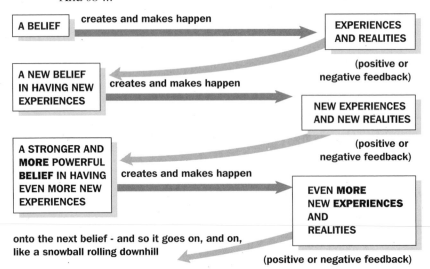

| A BELIEF | creates and makes happen | EXPERIENCES AND REALITIES |

(positive or negative feedback)

| A NEW BELIEF IN HAVING NEW EXPERIENCES | creates and makes happen | NEW EXPERIENCES AND NEW REALITIES |

(positive or negative feedback)

| A STRONGER AND **MORE** POWERFUL **BELIEF** IN HAVING EVEN MORE NEW EXPERIENCES | creates and makes happen | EVEN **MORE** NEW **EXPERIENCES** AND REALITIES |

onto the next belief - and so it goes on, and on, like a snowball rolling downhill

(positive or negative feedback)

☆   And so ...

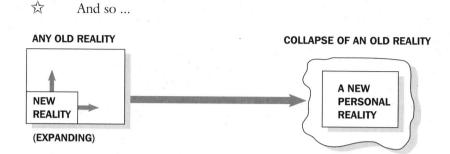

Change and disorder occur when any new reality violates the limits of any old reality. A person usually experiences confusion, doubt or uncertainty as any new personal reality grows at the expense of, and replaces, an old reality. But this process is essential to growth, expansion, change and health.

You have a choice ...

★   **in each moment, you can believe from your past experiences or previously defined realities (which means your ability to create afresh is limited)**

or ...

☆   **you can create from an open perspective of unlimited choice in the present moment.**

EXAMPLES OF MENTAL HABITS THAT YOU MAY BE USING TO CONTINUALLY USING TO REDUCE YOUR ABILITY TO CREATE

Do you recognise yourself doing any of these?

1   Making no new choices or decisions about anything.

2   Claiming that you are not responsible for what you are experiencing.

3   Holding fixed views or limited expectations about "how things are now" and "how things are going to be".

4   Remaining focused on the significance of past events or experiences.

5   Thinking about and analysing things instead of feeling and experiencing each successive new moment.

6   Being unaware that certain kinds of beliefs you have may be stuck on automatic creation - instead of being consciously aware and deliberately choosing what to believe and experience.

CHAPTER 2.4

BELIEF PATTERNS, STRUCTURES AND STRENGTH

Belief patterns and cycles are a natural part of people's lives. They can be responsible for creating repeated or sequential experiences. They vary in time duration, content and direction according to a person's individual characteristics, circumstances, age, outlook, actions etc.

The key to breaking belief patterns and cycles is to change the foundational beliefs which hold the power, and to adjust or reset them accordingly, as you choose.

 EXERCISE FOR YOU TO DO

Exercise aim: to discover belief patterns and cycles.

What to do

1   Choose an item from the following:

☆   a close or meaningful relationship that started and finished

★   a project that started and finished

☆   a job or career that started and finished

★   an interest, hobby or pursuit that started and finished.

2   Write a single brief objective or factual report, of about 500 words, about what **actually happened.**

3   Now break the story down into segments or sequences and write out each section into the boxes on the next page, under a heading from the menu.

The timescale of days, months or years may vary.

4   Adjust the number of boxes to the number your story requires.

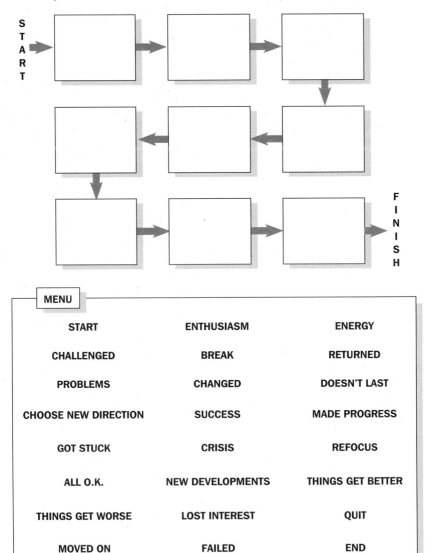

5   Add other descriptive and objective headings as required.

6   Now choose and complete belief patterns for all the other
     items above, so as to compare and contrast to see if there are
     similarities between your general belief life patterns and cycles.

7   Now examine the beliefs you held about each pattern at the
     beginning of each sequence.

> Jot down at least five beliefs you held at the
> beginning of each sequence.

> Jot down at least five beliefs you held
> at the end of each sequence.

8   Now consider whether there are **similar** beliefs
     present and actively influencing your major life experiences.

A COLLECTION OF BELIEFS

A person's collection of beliefs functions as a whole system, even allowing
for incoherent or dysfunctioning beliefs. Any belief system consists of a
host of individual beliefs that are held separately, but tend to have
influence together.

But it's not as simple as that; and there is not necessarily a clear
relationship between the two. Beliefs are often related and closely
associated and can, therefore, affect and influence each other. Any belief
changed or rearranged can influence the role of any or all of the other
beliefs.

It would be logical to assume that one belief would automatically create
one related specific experience:

| A BELIEF | creates | A RELATED EXPERIENCE |

An example:

A mixed collection of beliefs tends to create a mixed collection of experiences.

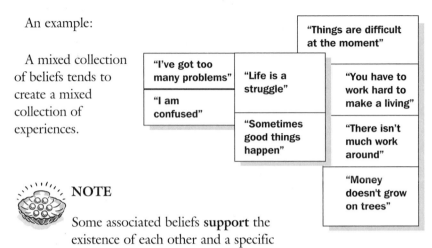

NOTE

Some associated beliefs **support** the existence of each other and a specific dominant belief. Some beliefs are more important and stronger (because they are believed to be more important) than other beliefs:

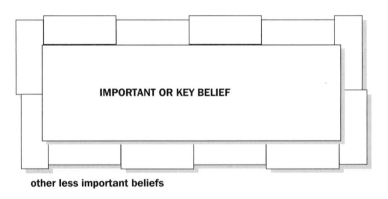

other less important beliefs

... and the beliefs used and lived through the most will tend to be most influential in a person's life.

HOW BELIEF STRUCTURES INFLUENCE WHAT YOU EXPERIENCE

Certain kinds of beliefs have more influence because of their nature and order of hierarchy or importance.

This diagram is a **generalised** model illustrating how certain kinds of beliefs tend to influence the functioning of each other:

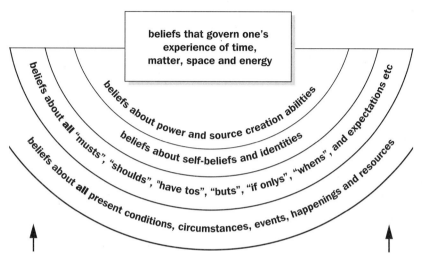

BELIEFS TEND TO APPEAR OR SURFACE TO ONE'S AWARENESS IN ASCENDING ORDER

WHAT CAN DETERMINE THE STRENGTH AND INFLUENCE OF A BELIEF?

1   The longer period of time a belief is held, the stronger it gets.

2   The amount to which a belief affects reality is determined by the measure of certainty and conviction with which it is held.

3   The amount of agreement and collusion between people about a belief.

Beliefs vary on a scale between "extremely doubtful" (or untrue) to being "absolutely true":

extremely doubtful or untrue   **absolutely true**

4   Conflicting beliefs held by the same person tend to cancel out each other's influence:

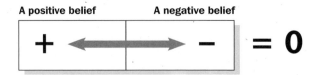

5   Having doubts and fears (which are a lack of belief and faith) automatically reduces the power and influence of beliefs.

6   **Beliefs believed with feeling and emotion are normally stronger and more influential than those casually believed.**

CHAPTER 2.5

BELIEF VARIABLES

Belief variables can affect the way beliefs can create and how they are experienced. The most influential belief variables are

Resistance

Flow

Desire

Change

Ease

Difficulty

Complexity

Simplicity

There may be other belief variables.

RESISTANCE

Situations in life can become resisted when one casts fixed labels or judgements upon them - instead of experiencing them fully with feeling. The solution is to release your judgements, which increases ease, flow and change in your life. This can assist and allow relief from resisted or stuck situations.

Resistance usually occurs by either

☆ not acknowledging being responsible for one's creations

or

★   having various kinds of beliefs that separate one from source awareness and one's own natural ability to create.

Things people commonly resist include

☆   change

★   their own feelings

☆   being themselves

(see Chapter 2.8, "Creating experiences with beliefs").

 EXERCISE FOR YOU TO DO

What are the things and situations in life you resist?

Take lots of time to contemplate this question! Come back to it often - it's not always easy to spot resistances - they have a way of hiding, because the old, stuck, psyche has an investment in keeping old resistances in place. Perhaps they were once useful, and maybe your psyche created them for very good reasons, and your old self feels comfortable with them. But maybe they're not appropriate or useful any more for today's, or tomorrow's, life ...

FLOW

Life always creates a natural flow of energy and change. If you don't resist, the flow of life will assist you in all matters.

EXAMPLE

There's a Chinese story of a water-beetle who lived on the riverbed, whose habit was to hang on grimly to a rock to avoid being swept along by the current. He was battered and bruised by the swirling waters, and he was unhappy. Another water-beetle, fed up with hurting, decided to let go, and was swept away, surrendering to the flowing water which carried him over and around the sharp rocks. As long as he didn't try to hang on, he remained unhurt. He was carried to the infinite ocean, where he attained happiness and fulfilment.

 KEY INSIGHT

☆ Create with the flow of life.

 EXERCISE FOR YOU TO DO

Take some time to contemplate what it feels like to mentally let go of some of the things you may be overattached to. What might be some results of that letting-go?

If you like, make some notes.

DESIRE

A desire is about wanting to experience or have something. Most people have healthy and natural desires; but there are of course some that are unhealthy.

 EXERCISE FOR YOU TO DO

Exercise aim: to test whether your desires are healthy.

Expected result: clarity about one's desires.

List your desires.

Your desires are healthy if they satisfy these questions:

1   Does what I desire benefit my welfare?

2   Does what I desire benefit the welfare of others?

3   Is what I desire an expression of love?

NOTE

☆   Honour your true desires.

★   Desire is an emotional energy with attractive qualities which will draw things to you.

☆   Some spiritual disciplines teach that desire is unhealthy and that it is best to have no desires at all - but the new desire to have no desire is just a replacement or displacement desire!

★   Desire and resistance can cancel each other out, leading to frustration! Having conflicting beliefs can thwart attaining what you desire.

CHANGE

There are only two constant factors in life: change, and source awareness; as LIFE seems to consist of a constantly vibrating and changing molecular energy force field.

Your beliefs about change will influence your experience of change.

Sometimes change can come about through ceasing to do over-complicated or self-sabotaging things.

 EXERCISE FOR YOU TO DO

Note down your beliefs about change.

Do you accept change easily?

 NOTE

★   If you believe you have the power and ability to adapt easily to change, then that is what you will experience.

EASE

Your beliefs about how easy something is will influence your experience of it.

 EXERCISE FOR YOU TO DO

List all the things you believe and experience as being easy in your life.

DIFFICULTY

Your beliefs about how difficult something is will influence your experience of it.

 EXERCISE FOR YOU TO DO

List all the things you believe and experience as being difficult in your life.

COMPLEXITY

Your beliefs about how complex something is will influence your experience of it.

 EXERCISE FOR YOU TO DO

List all the things you believe and experience as being complicated in your life.

SIMPLICITY

Your beliefs about how simple something is will influence your experience of it.

 EXERCISE FOR YOU TO DO

List all the things you believe and experience as being simple in your life.

PRESENT TIME, PAST AND FUTURE

The present moment is the only time you can experience. The past is gone and the future has not yet begun. Each moment of time is unique. Through and within the present moment, you can have the power and magic to create what you want. Only by using the present moment can you set the basis for the rest of your life.

Now is the only time that there **is**. Our perception of chronological or linear time records each successive instant moving onto the next, like lots of present moments strung together:

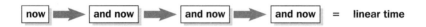

Through the present moment, unlimited possibilities can evolve, unfold and be unlocked.

VIEWPOINTS

☆   All beliefs held by a person all exist in present time. They are either continually recreated or carried over from one present moment to another, no matter how distant in the past these beliefs were originally created.

★   The past is a concept recreated through the present moment to serve as an explanation for the judgements and beliefs we have, or for the justification of the feelings we sometimes experience.

☆   All memories may be vivid to the recollector. But they can only be recalled **through** present time.

★   **The past can only influence you to the degree you believe that it is able to do so.**

☆ You can only create (for the future) in present time.

★ Time is a valuable commodity - use it well.

 KEY INSIGHTS

☆ **All beliefs function in present time ...**

... even if they are about the **past** or the **future**.

★ In the present moment you have the power to choose your thoughts, beliefs and actions. Present time can shape your future.

 EXERCISE FOR YOU TO DO

What beliefs do you have about what you experience as time? Jot them down.

 VIEWPOINT

Perceptions of time vary. Have you noticed how time seems to fly when you are enjoying yourself? Likewise, how time seems to drag when you are doing something you don't enjoy?

EXERCISE FOR YOU TO DO

1   Find somewhere remote (preferably with a good view) where you can be alone for a while. Contemplate for a while:

☆ short, long and infinite spans of time

★ whether you perceive yourself to be separate from your experience of time.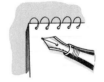

2   Consider what you feel about time and how it influences your life. Jot down your thoughts and feelings about it.

3   Consider the concept that present time can only happen because infinite time (and space) exists. Jot down your thoughts and feelings about it.

CHAPTER 2.7

THE EXPERIENCE OF REALITY

We experience what is real for us, and what is real for us is created by the beliefs we hold.

In effect, everyone lives within their own "belief" worlds, even though they may be shared, interconnected or joined to other people's worlds or realities. Multiple realities and worlds exist - how else can two people experience the same event totally differently?

What is real in the world is essentially a separate question. Life has many dimensions of infinite variety and diversity. There even seem to be worlds within worlds - from the subatomic molecular level to the infinite never-ending universe of billions of galaxies ... .

When no judgements are placed on reality as you experience it, you can view it freshly "just as it is", or "how it is" ...

How any individual experiences the world as it is, rests upon the overall content, arrangement and make-up of the collection of beliefs they hold. Anyone can create possibilities by believing themselves into them, and can dissolve any limitations by believing (and then experiencing) themselves out of them. However, conflicts can arise when imagined high expectations are placed on the mundane realities of everyday life.

And so, to the extent that they fail to manage their beliefs, reality remains beyond their influence - out of reach of their creation, direction and overall control. Therefore, reality **is** what is individually **real** for each person, and that varies according to each person.

 KEY INSIGHT

 ★ Beliefs about reality create how reality is experienced.

There are no universal laws of human nature, experience and behaviour that say that these things are fixed or constant. Life just **is**. It doesn't have its own meaning - we create that! - although the **purpose** of life for some people is probably to evolve, creating more efficient, simpler and higher-quality things. (But the purpose of life is probably different for every individual.)

EXERCISE FOR YOU TO DO

Take some time alone to think about what you have just read. Then contemplate these questions, and use your journal to write your reflections. (Some people have problems because they confuse reality with imagined reality.)

1   Are you happy with your life as it is now?

2   If you are unhappy, what is it that you are unhappy about?

3   What beliefs do you have about this situation?

    Remember that by releasing any judgements or prejudice (prejudgements) or beliefs you have about "how your life is now", you can allow it to change for the better.

4   Is your life within your overall direction and control most of the time?/some of the time?/not at all?

5   What beliefs do you have about the effectiveness of your ability to create the kinds of experiences and circumstances you desire?

6   What beliefs do you have about you **not** being able to experience that you are creating your experiences?

7   What beliefs do you have about reality? Is your life restricted in any way? Do you have the right conditions and adequate resources to do what you want?

8   What beliefs do you have about your ability to exist in the world?

9   On a scale of 1 to 10, how confident and certain are you that you can create or cause to happen the kinds of events, circumstances and experiences you desire?

10   On a scale of 1 to 10, mark the degree of direct connection you consider there to be between what you think and believe, and what happens in your life.

completely uncertain about any connection   **1** ————————→ **10**   absolutely certain about there being a direct definite connection

11   In what, or where, does the dominant or deciding power and control of your life reside?

12   What do you believe is possible for you to do, be, or have?

13   What do you believe is impossible for you to do, be, or have?

14   What or who limits you from having, doing or being anything you desire?

15   What pressures or troubles (if any) are you facing and experiencing in your life now?

16   What beliefs do you have that create these pressures you experience?

NOTE

★   Many of our beliefs about reality and what is possible or impossible contain important but invisible self-limitations which affect our experience of change, possibilities, resources, time and space. Growth and change means living beyond what our personal concepts of reality are.

☆ If some, all, many or most limitations are self-imposed or made up, they can be discreated or dissolved in the same way they were originally created. For it is possible that reality can contain an infinite number of limitless possibilities, if only we can expand and change our beliefs to be open enough to experience them.

KEY INSIGHT

★ Some limitations to the realities we experience are self-created and self-imposed.

EXERCISE FOR YOU TO DO

Contemplate and answer as completely and as fully as you can:

My life is ...

CREATING EXPERIENCES WITH BELIEFS

You can create experiences with beliefs effortlessly and easily without conflict as long as

1   there are no pre-existing beliefs

2   you choose **one** viewpoint from which to create; problems and conflicts can arise if you hold and switch between two or more viewpoints

3   you remain with that viewpoint until you have created what you want.

Changing your life or your reality begins with changing your viewpoint or perspective - your relationship to what you are creating and experiencing. This can be enhanced by identifying and changing the ways labels of definition are placed on creations and experiences.

The relationship between creating and experiencing what you believe happens in cycles or waves, rather like breathing in and out. You need to experience fully what you have already created, because if you resist experiencing, you'll lose clarity and ability.

When resisted experiences build up and don't get cleared, they become energy that creates such things as problems, obstacles, or stubborn (resistant to change) situations that start to take over and govern your life. In extreme cases, matters get out of control.

Any experience can get resisted until you fully experience it with **appreciation** and **acceptance**. For example, if you are resisting experiencing the absence or lack of something, you need to appreciate this lack - and then you'll find that the resistance changes to flow - and you can experience different circumstances and be able to move forward.

SOME FURTHER HAZARDS TO CREATING

1   Trying to quickly create or change something **in reaction** to what

you have just created with your pre-existing beliefs.

2   Changing your point of view (viewpoints) as you create.

3   Having fixed or rigid expectations instead of positive flexible expectations.

4   Trying to pressurise or force some outcome, in order to avoid some other undesired outcome from happening.

5   Pretending instead of creating.

 VIEWPOINTS

Here are a couple of definitions to highlight the difference between creating and pretending.

CREATING - is imagination **with** faith and belief.

PRETENDING - is imagination **without** faith and belief.

DISBELIEF - is believing that you don't believe something.

It takes effort to pretend something - trying to experience something unreal or not genuine, or displaying something different from what one truly believes or feels. People who believe in their pretences usually create them for real.

FEAR   *is a belief founded in your own inadequacy and a perception or belief about some experience or reality seen as being greater than one's ability to change, accept or overcome it.*

"In-ad-equacy", from the Latin, means being **not equal or up to** something - not able to deal with, face, or overcome something.

Fears, though, can be about anything specific or non-specific (like phobias or obsessions). But fears faced and acknowledged with honesty usually disperse.

Many of our fears and hurts are primarily caused by

★   our own judgements of ourselves

☆   creating others who hurt us emotionally.

The mind holds beliefs about the judgements **and** the hurt.

COURAGE

is an attitude of feeling, meaning you are able to deal with anything.

HOPE

means to entertain a wish for something with some expectation.

DOUBT

is a conflict between old and new decisions, or a conflict of choice between two or more current ones.

CONFUSION

is the enemy of clear thinking and mental abilities. It is usually caused by conflicts between beliefs, priorities or goals.

WORRY

means having a fearful or anxious focus on some matter.

★ All believing and creating is on-going!

However, sometimes the original belief that a person has created something with has become lost or hidden:

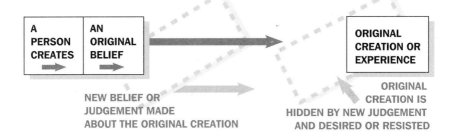

When a person disowns - does not claim authorship - for their experiences by denying they created it, or through memory lapse, invalidation or judgement, **the original substance of the first belief and creation/experience continues to exist by default ...**

So ...

1   Any overlaid additional beliefs and judgements which determine what is perceived as good or bad, ugly or beautiful, right or wrong etc, react against the original belief, which is experienced as either

☆   wanted - desired, or unwanted - resisted

in relation to the original belief.

2   The more overlaid or layered an original belief becomes, the harder it is to create through it.

3   A person who constantly changes their viewpoint or perspective and adds judgements on top of any creation is likely to experience additional confusion and random events containing mixed results, whilst the original belief goes unaddressed, unrecognised and unchanged.

4   A similar pattern of resisted events is likely to repeat itself when fundamental personal beliefs remain unchanged over a period of time. For example, some people experience consistent patterns of relationship problems, financial difficulties and unwanted situations reoccurring in their life.

VIEWPOINT

When you get to a point where you are able to effortlessly accept and appreciate all your creations, you'll find it much easier to discover and access your original and core beliefs. Then real change on a very deep level can happen easily.

But if you deny authorship of your creations and experiences, you may have to experience powerlessness and to struggle with creations and experiences that resist change, even though you created them initially. This is, in effect, using your own power to render yourself powerless.

CHANGING BELIEFS

To change your beliefs you need to

1 *locate and identify your current or original beliefs that can get hidden under overlaid layers of beliefs*

2 *unravel complicated beliefs*

3 *realign your major beliefs*

4 *discreate, dissolve or release unwanted beliefs*

5 *create new replacement or alternative beliefs.*

1 LOCATING AND IDENTIFYING YOUR CURRENT BELIEFS

It is essential and important to change the right belief **before** creating a new one, otherwise you would just create another belief conflict.

The beliefs you already hold fit into and mirror the experiences and circumstances you already have in your life.

The outlines in this chapter are intended to help you to discover and examine your present deep beliefs. Once you have found them, these beliefs should

1 provide you with some further understanding of their cause-and-effect relationship

2   feel right and appropriately "real" to you

3   be useful in evaluating your own beliefs - see Section 4, "Discovering and examining your own beliefs".

 NOTE

It is usually the older on-going and persistent (sometimes invisible and unrecognised) beliefs that often create most of the problems a person has.

2 UNRAVELLING COMPLICATED BELIEFS

... is essential if a person had a wide and conflicting variety of beliefs present in one or all areas of their life.

Choose simple beliefs that work well for you.

3 REALIGNING YOUR MAJOR BELIEFS

... is best achieved by reassessing your most important dreams and goals, and making sure that these are in a parallel supporting relationship. To realign your goals and beliefs, see Section 5, "New possibilities - creating your future".

4 DISCREATING, DISSOLVING OR RELEASING YOUR UNWANTED BELIEFS

... is an important step before changing or creating new beliefs. Because if you leave this step out, the old beliefs will continue to have power and influence in your life, and there tends to be little new or additional space for a new belief to be influential, without creating a new and additional conflict with a pre-existing belief. When an old (redundant, but still present) or current belief conflicts with a new belief forced upon it (see the diagram below), mixed results occur, with the older stronger belief normally prevailing and reasserting its dominance. This explains how some people try to change their lives in this manner, but usually return to the unwanted original situations again.

A new belief being forced upon a present or old belief leads to

☆ mixed results and experiences

★ belief conflicts

☆ the present or old belief remaining influential.

On the other hand, creating, dissolving or releasing a present or old belief creates the space that enables a new belief to be successful:

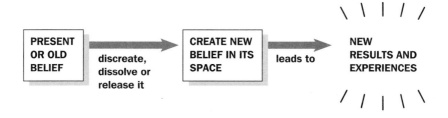

To discreate, dissolve or release a belief, you need to

★ know what it is

☆ feel it, be it, see it

★ use your natural ability to disempower it by stopping believing in it

☆ use any form of symbolic visualisation to assist in rubbing out or diminishing an unwanted belief ...

An unwanted belief is usually held subconsciously (out of your everyday awareness), and once you bring full conscious awareness to it, it is relatively easy to start deliberately choosing to believe otherwise.

The subconscious mind really does act on the clear suggestions and instructions you give to it; the unwanted belief may persist unless addressed at this deep level.

☆   use your awareness to discover how you created your original belief creation during some moment in the past.

5 CREATING NEW BELIEFS

The key to **creating new beliefs** is to

★   CHOOSE OR MAKE UP WHATEVER YOU WANT TO BELIEVE FROM ABSOLUTELY ANYTHING. YOU CAN BELIEVE WHATEVER YOU WANT! THE NOTION OF "I DECIDE" CAN FREE YOU FROM ANY ADDICTION TO FORMULAS OR ANSWERS.

It is best for a new belief to be in supporting harmony with other beliefs you already have. For some people, whose majority of beliefs have been indoctrinated or conditioned into them by other people or social organisations, **this may involve changing the habits of an entire lifetime.** Having discreated any old or unwanted beliefs, you should be able to easily find the space within your mind to create a new belief that can now create new experiences and circumstances, without conflict or clutter.

 SUMMARY

1   SUSPEND ALL DISBELIEF AND CREATE YOUR NEW BELIEF.

2   START BELIEVING IN YOUR NEW BELIEF.

3   GIVE IT FOCUS, ENERGY AND ATTENTION.

4   BELIEVE IT WITH FEELING, AS IF IT WERE ALREADY TRUE.

5   SEE WHAT HAPPENS AS A RESULT!

SECTION 3
SELF-BELIEFS AND IDENTITY

3.1   SELF-BELIEFS AND IDENTITY
3.2   SELF-ESTEEM
3.3   SELF-CONFIDENCE
3.4   SELF-WORTH
3.5   SELF-ACCEPTANCE AND SELF-LOVE

*"For a man to achieve all that is demanded of him,
he must regard himself greater than he is."*

Johann W von Goethe (1749 - 1832)
German scientist and literary figure.

*"To be, or not to be -
that is the question ..."*   *Hamlet*

William Shakespeare (1564 - 1616)

*My light
comes from my
self-beliefs.*

Self-beliefs and identity

There is absolutely no substitute for the magic of **believing in yourself**. This is an important and central belief that enables all other beliefs to function in your favour.

Strong positive self-beliefs create quality characteristics in people such as charisma, beauty, poise, presence, charm and sex appeal.

 KEY INSIGHT

★ **You cannot have or maintain any creation or experience unless you possess enough relative self-belief to sustain it.**

For example:

You cannot cook an excellent meal unless you have the necessary ingredients **and** enough self-belief in yourself and your ability to do so.

Who, what, and how you are, are likewise also made up from belief definitions about yourself. These are called **identities**, or **selves**, and these directly affect your general state of being and the overall quality of your life experiences. Self-belief problems often arise out of conflict between the imposed and conditioned beliefs about who or what you **should** be, with who or what you really are or want to be.

 KEY INSIGHTS

☆ Source awareness creates or empowers any identity, self-belief or collection of beliefs imposed on it.

★ Source **awareness** plus **definition** equals **identity**.

☆ All **definitions** of self, identity or being are all products of belief, usually characterised by "**I am ...**" beliefs.

★ All identities and selves contain sets of beliefs that are **more** influential than **most** other forms of belief because they are of a higher order. That is, they are more important and stronger.

 EVIDENCE

☆ You can only perceive or experience any reality **through** some self-belief or definition.

★ All identities or selves determine what is perceived and how it is perceived in any reality.

Furthermore, **any** identity or self is created by a collection or set of defining beliefs. Therefore, the more defined the belief, the more defined the identity; and therefore, the more flexible the belief, the more flexible the identity.

For example:

☆ a **defined** identity - "I **am** a policeman"

★ a **flexible** identity - "I **am** a sociable person"

 KEY INSIGHTS

☆ Each identity or self has its own set of beliefs.

★ Some identities or selves **conflict** with each other, whilst others **reinforce** each other.

☆ Identities and selves are either

asserted - what you want to be

resisted - what you don't want to be.

★ Contradictions and conflicts within an identity or self tend to neutralise each other.

Any set of beliefs that define an identity, or label it in a particular way, when believed by a person, tend to become real and meaningful. Certain collective identities, held by large groups of people, have been the source of much conflict in the world. These identities include those based on

☆ nationality

★ race

☆ religious customs and beliefs

★ political ideologies and creeds.

Other identities or belief labels commonly found are

★ status and social role

☆ ability

★ power

☆ wealth

★ age

☆ sexuality.

EXAMINING DIFFERENT FORMS OF IDENTITY

There are two main forms of identity that can be distinguished and defined in the following ways:

1   A deliberate identity

These can be made up as one creates it, and used for as long as desired, rather like an actor playing a role.

2   A persistent identity

These identities were created at some point in the past and they continue to persist and are usually dependent and resistant to conscious and deliberate control.

Persistent identities seem so familiar to the creator and holder that they are rarely examined and changed because they are the building blocks of who you believe yourself to be. Contemplating changing these identities can evoke uncertainty and fear!

WHAT IDENTITIES DO

They serve to filter, interpret and stimulate one's experience of life. They judge what is good or bad, right or wrong, what creates satisfaction or disappointment.

★   They create **meaning**.

☆   They determine what is possible for each person.

★   They determine levels of achievement.

☆   They determine body appearance, performance, health and disease.

★   They are **usually** (but not always) the source of unwelcome experiences!

KEY INSIGHTS

☆   Identities can only be changed by the original creator. So, the key is to work to get the persistent identities to entertain change or transformation.

By teaching identities how to change and build new belief structures, **resistant** identities can be evolved into **deliberate** identities, and greater flexibility achieved in one's state of being. When a person is wearing a "being" belief it can dominate their state of being.

EXERCISE FOR YOU TO DO

Exercise aim: to explore the definitions you are currently imposing on your awareness about yourself.

Intended result: to gain insights and relief from any fixed conditions you are experiencing.

Take a short time to write about each of the topics listed below, in the form beginning "**I am** ...". Be sure to write **spontaneous** answers!

health	status	
nationality	importance	perseverance
profession	education	sensitivity
ability	reputation	ambition
reliability	gender	deserving
finance	relationships	luck
size	sexuality	religion
attitude	courage	beauty

Now, for **each** item, consider which of the following applies to each response. You might like to put a number (1 to 4) alongside each topic you wrote about, so you can compare quickly.

Is it ...

1   deliberately chosen by yourself?

2   deliberately modelled on something or someone else?

3   chosen in obedience to someone else's expectation of you?

4   chosen in a reaction to someone else, or someone else's opinion?

 CONSIDER

Have most of your self-definition beliefs been acquired from other people rather than created by yourself?

 EXERCISE FOR YOU TO DO

Exercise aim: to define self-definitions based upon what you are **not**.

Intended result: to clarify how you define yourself using negative definitions.

Consider how you define yourself by what you are **not**, and jot down four or five definitions (or however many).

 EXERCISE FOR YOU TO DO

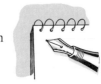

Define who you believe yourself to be (in about 100 words).

 EXERCISE FOR YOU TO DO

Exercise aim: to discover your most negative beliefs about yourself.

Expected result: relief from these conditions.

Think of the five worst things about yourself and write them down. (Remember you don't have to show this to anyone!) Then write what **evidence** there is to support each belief.

Now let's finish by a final bit of self-examination ...

 CONSIDER

Is there one underlying negative belief about yourself that tends to support the existence of, and confirm, all the others? Write down:

My most negative belief about myself is...

... though having said all that ...

There is no need to let your current state of being get in the way of what you might become. Changing your most negative belief about yourself can have a positive effect on your well-being!

SOME USEFUL BEING BELIEFS ARE...

To be ...

☆ whole

★ healthy

☆ true to yourself

★ fully alive in every moment of time

☆ the determining power in your life

★ free to choose

☆ happy and fulfilled

★ able to learn and change.

 IN SUMMARY

The possible answer to the question "Who am I?" is probably - whatever or whoever you want to be, as you are the one who decides, or has decided.

Identities or self-beliefs function together under the following principles. They can be

☆ in harmony with each other and support each other

or

★   in conflict with each other

or

☆   be detached and separated from each other.

By bringing all identities together in wholeness of function, conflicting self-beliefs, self-judgements and identities are removed. For example, any identity calling itself "good" that casts judgement on a "bad" self or identity, disallows or disallows integration of both identities. By removing self-judgement, one's true nature can be expressed and experienced.

There are, however, private, secret or hidden identities (of any kind) which are sometimes called the dark side of human nature. These can be influential in determining someone's personality. However, human nature can change, and any negative or destructive identities can be transformed and brought into alignment and harmony with the best emotional qualities and values a person holds in their heart.

SELF-ESTEEM

SELF-ESTEEM - pride in oneself, self-respect

SELF-CONSCIOUS - aware of oneself or one's own being, actions or thoughts

Everyone needs self-esteem, or self-regard. It's an essential part in believing in yourself because it reflects the **amount** of personal liking for yourself that you have, plus the **way** you feel good about yourself and the life you lead.

Self-esteem is a reflection of the type of feelings you have for yourself, and your opinion of yourself. As described in Chapter 3.1, "Self-beliefs and identity", different selves or identities usually have differing levels of self-esteem. In this way, self-esteem is relative to the presence, nature and function of all self-beliefs.

Highly successful people possess ALL five of these essential attributes:

1   **they have high self-esteem**

2   **they take responsibility for themselves, their actions, and their lives**

3   **they have specific goals they want to achieve next**

4   **they are persistent and never give up on their dreams and desires**

5   **they associate with other successful people similar to themselves.**

Levels of self-esteem affect

★   the amount of self-confidence or belief in yourself that you have

☆   your personal effectiveness and your abilities

★ the overall self-image or inner mental picture you have that details what you believe yourself to be like

☆ your emotional well-being and health, and the quality of your experiences or feelings.

As a general rule, people can feel good about themselves in direct proportion to the general amount of control and autonomy they have in their lives.

With a large amount of control over one's life, it is easier to feel good about oneself. But if you have little or no influence or control over your life, events can reflect and lead to low self-esteem, stress, and the lack of emotional well-being.

Self-esteem has an inverse relationship to stress levels. High stress levels experienced by a person reflect low self-esteem, and high self-esteem can lower stress levels.

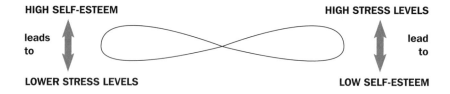

HIGH SELF-ESTEEM   **HIGH STRESS LEVELS**

leads to   lead to

LOWER STRESS LEVELS   **LOW SELF-ESTEEM**

SO WHAT FACTORS CAN LOWER SELF-ESTEEM?

Any negative self-belief that allows people to feel bad about themselves and ...

★ too much stress

☆ repeated failures and unfulfilled goals

★ disappointments

☆ disasters

★ having a low opinion of oneself

☆ relationship breakdowns

★ illness

☆ drugs

★ bereavement

☆ being under constant pressure

★ financial difficulties

☆ being trapped in unwanted situations

★ powerlessness
and hopelessness

☆ criticism from
others

★ self-criticism

☆ guilt and shame

★ abiding by
others' wishes at
the expense of
your own.

The amount of self-esteem a person has is relative to the nature and function of their self-beliefs. Each identity or self has its own amount or level of self-esteem incorporated within it.

For example:

★ a person can be an excellent musician, but a poor cook

☆ a person can be an excellent driver, but a poor business partner.

Every role, identity or self that a person has, has its own level of self-esteem, independent of each other. This is why people can experience mild versions of the "Jekyll and Hyde" personality phenomenon.

As different self-beliefs have their own qualities of self-esteem, the **overall** level of self-esteem experienced by any person is averaged out between the different selves, roles or identities:

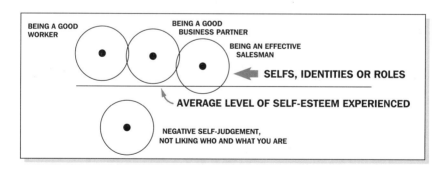

OBSERVATIONS

1   In the diagram above, you can see that the average level of self-esteem experienced by the person is reduced because there is one self much lower than the rest.

2   With different self-beliefs possessing large differences in self-esteem, a person is likely to experience oscillating and sometimes uncontrollable emotional moods of highs and lows!

3   The most effective way of raising a person's average level of self-esteem is to raise the **lowest level first!**

In contrast, a person with broadly similar levels of self-esteem within each self, role or identity ...

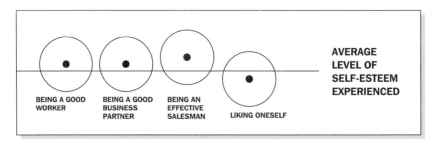

AVERAGE
LEVEL OF
SELF-ESTEEM
EXPERIENCED

BEING A GOOD WORKER   BEING A GOOD BUSINESS PARTNER   BEING AN EFFECTIVE SALESMAN   LIKING ONESELF

... is more likely to have mostly stable and healthy emotional experiences.

 KEY INSIGHT

★ **Identifying** and **raising** one's self-beliefs that contain the lowest or most negative levels of self-esteem is the best way to raise the overall, or average, level of self-esteem. See Chapter 3.5, "Self-acceptance and self-love".

SELF-CONFIDENCE

SELF-CONFIDENCE - confidence in oneself or one's abilities

SELF-DOUBT - a lack of faith, belief or confidence in oneself

Self-confidence is almost the same as believing in yourself, and is closely associated with self-esteem. Self-confidence is a measure of the amount you believe in yourself and your skills, abilities and talents, irrespective of what circumstances you face in your life.

Self-confidence can be eroded and diminished in a way similar to how self-esteem gets lowered. But **failure, fear** and **self-doubt** can play a more significant role in denting self-confidence.

Self-confidence is something that usually gets built up in steps over a period of time, and unshakable self-confidence is one of the very best possessions anyone can have in life, alongside peace of mind.

 EXERCISE FOR YOU TO DO

Write your responses to this statement:

My greatest shortcomings are ...

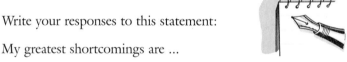

Now have a look at this diagram and mark the scale as to roughly where you think you are on it.

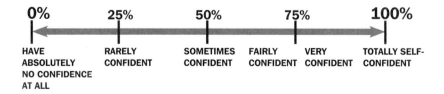

0%	25%	50%	75%	100%
HAVE ABSOLUTELY NO CONFIDENCE AT ALL	RARELY CONFIDENT	SOMETIMES CONFIDENT	FAIRLY CONFIDENT VERY CONFIDENT	TOTALLY SELF-CONFIDENT

Now write down ...

Some simple things I can do now to gradually build up my self-confidence are ...

Most self-beliefs interact and function together, influencing each other:

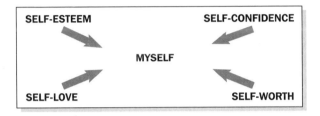

SELF-ESTEEM   **SELF-CONFIDENCE**

MYSELF

SELF-LOVE   **SELF-WORTH**

KEY INSIGHT

☆ Improving the lowest or weakest part of your self-beliefs will influence and lift all the other parts.

SELF-WORTH

SELF-WORTH is related to self-esteem. It is both

★   **a measure of the amount of worthiness you place upon yourself, being special and unique, and**

☆   **a reflection of the relative value you place upon yourself, your time, your talents, your abilities and your resources.**

Positive self-worth also allows and creates value, honour and standards of good treatment to and from other people. Having high self-worth and high self-esteem makes it far easier to create quality life experiences.

VIEWPOINTS

1   In childhood and adolescence, people are taught certain indirect and implied lessons - by school, society and family - more about what they cannot do, rather than what they can.

2   When conditional rewarding systems are used to influence the behaviour of children - such as "if you are good then you can have this" or "if you misbehave you'll have to go without" - and these rewards and punishments are repeated, the child learns and begins to believe that they have to be good enough (in some way) to deserve and get what they want.

3   When the use of the withdrawal of love and approval is administered as a tool to manage children's behaviour, this can create certain kinds of self-beliefs that can cause children difficulties in adult life.

4   Any conditioning or experiences that cause a child to continually doubt their own self-worth, or to believe themselves to be unworthy or not good enough in any way, may account for some of the unfulfilled lives some people have. Any conditions to be placed upon parental love and support can cast a question-mark over a person's

basic and inherent worthiness and state of being.

 NOTE

Having very healthy self-worth means that you believe you are **unconditionally** worthy and deserving of having, doing or being all of your dreams and goals - for absolutely **no** reason at all!

This is a far healthier foundational belief to have than anything else. This positive belief can diminish the conditional need to have to work excessively hard and struggle for things in life.

EXERCISE FOR YOU TO DO

Exercise aim: to reflect on the degree to which you **actually** value yourself in various ways.

Contemplate and jot down:

What value do you place on yourself?

What value do you place on your talents, abilities and skills?

What value do you place on your time?

Now, let's move on. Take as long as you like to contemplate this next bit. In fact, it would be good to dwell on it.

★ **What would it actually feel like to be unconditionally worthy and deserving of having, doing or being all of your dreams and goals? (Remember, you can imagine being in this state now!)**

Self-acceptance and self-love

SELF-ACCEPTANCE means

☆ **not judging yourself**

★ **accepting completely who and exactly how you are now.**

Through and by self-acceptance, you can allow what you believe and experience about yourself to change. **Any** self-judgement has the power keep you locked into experiencing persistent unwanted conditions. Self-acceptance is the doorway to change and is the solution to getting fixed judgements and resistances to shift out of the way.

Society today - our culture at large - does not easily advocate or endorse self-love. It is viewed suspiciously, and mistakenly, for narcissism, selfishness or arrogance. And yet, as an emotional quality derived from a belief, it is very important and beneficial.

 VIEWPOINTS

Reasons for loving yourself more include:

☆ The more you love yourself, the more you are able to love other people. It can be difficult to give to others something that you do not possess yourself.

★ When you love yourself you are acknowledging the true divine nature that is within you, and all that is in life. If you do not love yourself properly you deny your own nature to the world.

☆ When you love yourself you can feel at one with other people more easily. Each of us is a unique individual being, yet we all seem to be connected. If you can't love yourself adequately, you continue to support the belief-pattern that you will always remain separate or isolated.

☆   Taking responsibility for yourself and all of your life is easier with self-love. It is also simpler to follow your highest purpose, even though you may have to take risks and face some of your own fears.

★   From self-love flows self-acceptance, self-forgiveness, greater joy, and inner peace.

EXERCISE FOR YOU TO DO

Take some time alone. Using a mirror, look closely into your own eyes and repeat slowly and sincerely for several minutes:

"I love you, just the way you are."

How did this make you feel?

Did you experience thoughts of disbelief, or any negative feelings? Any "yuk!"? What objections do you have to the question? (It might be interesting in the future to look back at your journal to this time to see what you wrote!)

But whatever your responses at this time now, the mirror technique can be very good for you. It

☆   is direct and effective when used regularly

★   can increase self-acceptance and self-love

☆   can disarm your normal resistance to loving yourself unconditionally.

The technique can also be easily adapted by using different phrases or questions, a larger mirror, and with other (or no) styles of clothing and dress.

Some ways self-love gets denied include

★   taking yourself too seriously

☆   feeling unworthy

★ negative self-judgements of any kind

☆ being a perfectionist! - trying too hard to be perfect or good enough, because one may believe one is not

★ being an idealist, trying to live to high expectations and impossible standards.

Why not ...?

Love yourself, believe in yourself, trust your feelings and intuition, follow your heart, decide on what you really want, and resolve to act and do it now!

SECTION 4
DISCOVERING AND EXAMINING YOUR OWN BELIEFS

4.1   TRUTH AND HONESTY

4.2   WHAT IS REALLY IMPORTANT TO YOU - AND WHY?

4.3   EVERYDAY FUNCTIONAL BELIEFS

4.4   HIDDEN AND INVISIBLE BELIEFS

4.5   BELIEF COUNSELLING APPROACHES

4.6   BELIEFS, FEELINGS, VALUES AND ATTITUDES

4.7   ALIVENESS AND WELL-BEING BELIEFS

4.8   SHORT-TERM AND LONG-TERM BELIEFS

4.9   GENETIC, CULTURAL AND GROUP BELIEFS

4.10 ALLOWANCES AND OTHER BELIEFS

*"His passions make Man live,
his wisdom makes him last."*

Chamfort
French philosospher.

I can discover
the treasures
of belief
within me.

TRUTH AND HONESTY

It is important to be truthful and honest with yourself about what you **truly** believe. Self-truth can reveal your true feelings and beliefs which can otherwise be hidden or disguised by what you **think** you should believe, or what you **want** to believe.

When you are examining the nature of your own beliefs, it's good to extend to yourself as much honesty as possible in everything you think and feel about yourself. If you are dishonest in this, there's a danger that your connection to source awareness may get reduced. You may then project dishonesty onto others around you, and in the world in general.

At times, though, it can be easier to shut off from other people, and the world in general, in order to protect one's dishonesties. Most people do this constantly, and unconsciously, and in varying degrees.

So by increasing your capacity to be honest within yourself, you can free up or release your attention. We're talking about the attention that might otherwise get fixed on protecting your secrets - in other words, your negative self-reflection. But don't worry - **everyone** has secrets!

But when this energy is released, more energy becomes available to you, and this can lead directly to empowering you to change and direct your life more successfully.

The next exercise is designed to increase your self-honesty and reduce any self-deceptions you may have.

 EXERCISE FOR YOU TO DO

Exercise aim: to recognise the ways you deceive yourself. It's time to get honest. Remember you don't have to show this to anyone if you don't want to.

1.   List three errors you frequently observe in others.

Now consider: are there times when you refuse to recognise these same errors in yourself?

2   List three actions you do in order to persuade other people to believe certain things about you.

Now consider: what is it that you **don't** believe about yourself that causes you to try and persuade another person to believe something about you?

3   List three conflicts that you are involved in.

Now consider: what beliefs do you have that may be responsible for creating the circumstances of these struggles?

4   List three experiences which seem to happen repeatedly in your life.

Now consider: what beliefs would you have to have in order to create these experiences?

WHAT IS REALLY IMPORTANT TO YOU - AND WHY?

It is not only **what** you believe that influences your life, but **how** you believe these beliefs.

What - means the content of your beliefs.

How - means the structure, order, alignment and relative strength of your beliefs.

Consider for a moment the point about **how** you believe your beliefs.

☆ What are the things that you hold to be the most important in your life?

★ Do you also give these things the highest priority in your everyday life?

It is far easier to create and to have a well-balanced, easily functioning life when you put first whatever matters most.

The opposite can also apply: quality life experiences may be difficult to sustain if you ignore or devalue what is truly important to you, at the expense of something else.

We've already made the point earlier on that it's so easy to take on from other people, or society at large, things that **should** be important for us. It's good to remind ourselves: outside influences give us lots of rules and regulations, oughts and shoulds, and are extremely powerful; and we can so easily forget that we can choose for **ourselves** what is important.

 EXERCISE FOR YOU TO DO

Exercise aim: to clarify what is important to you.

Take plenty of time to consider these questions, and jot down some answers.

1   What is really important to you?

2   And now, what is really important to you, about
      what is really important?

   For most people, what usually matters most to them
is love, other people, relationships, and other things that they value in
their heart.

 EXERCISE FOR YOU TO DO

   Exercise aim: to determine the existing order
   of importance of people or things in your life,
   as it is now.

★   Draw a chart with numbers 1 to 10 down the left, and put two
      column headings on the right-hand side, like this:

		IMPORTANCE POINTS	VALUE POINTS
1			
2			
3			
4			

☆   Down the left, list ten people, objects, issues, events or projects you
      have recently been interested in.

   Look down your list and assign **relative importance** to each item.

   Give each one a score, where

      1 means high importance, and
      10 means low importance.

Write it in the first column under the heading "Importance points".

★ Look down your list again and give a **value** to each item. Again, give each a score, where

1 means "I am perfectly happy with it", and
10 means "it is not right at all".

Put the score in the second column under the heading "Value points".

☆ Compare the two columns of points and see if there is any kind of correlation between them:

a   most high-importance points match high-value points
     (1s and 2s go together)

b   most high-importance points match low-value points
     (1s and 2s match 9s and 10s)

c   most low-importance points match high-value points
     (9s and 10s match 1s and 2s)

d   there is no obvious relationship between the two sets of points.

Now consider whether what is of importance to you is also of the highest priority. If it isn't, consider ways to adjust and change your life so that more priority is focused on what matters most.

CHAPTER 4.3

EVERYDAY FUNCTIONAL BELIEFS

Our general everyday beliefs directly affect the experiences we have.

Let's begin with an exercise to highlight the significance they have to you, personally.

 EXERCISE FOR YOU TO DO

Exercise aim: to determine the content and usefulness of everyday functional beliefs.

Take however long you like to consider these.

1 List four things you believe about your experience of money.

2 List four things you believe about your experience of work.

3 List four things you believe about your experience of other people in the world.

4 List four things you believe about your experience of what life is like.

5 List four things you believe about how the world is now.

6 List four things you believe about yourself today.

7 List four things you believe about your abilities.

8 List four things you believe about your past.

9 List four things you believe about your future.

10 List four things you believe about having, or not having, everything you require to achieve anything you want.

★ After each reply, add a plus (+) to denote whether this belief is helpful to you, or a minus (-) to signify it is unhelpful.

☆ Now mark each reply from a score of 1 point to denote whether you think the belief is extremely doubtful, to a maximum of 10 points to signify that this belief is absolutely true.

Now mark each reply with

X to represent a belief that was given to you or indoctrinated

✔ to represent a belief that you have chosen.

☆ Now examine each reply and replace the ones that you no longer want or like with some that you do!

HIDDEN AND INVISIBLE BELIEFS

Apart from the wide variety of self-beliefs and general everyday functional beliefs that we have already discussed so far in this book, there are certain other types of regularly active and frequently used beliefs.

These other beliefs are hidden, lost or invisible beliefs - they are present but not obvious at all. Some are helpful; and others can cause nothing but problems for the believer. Beliefs can become lost after goals are completed and/or after goals change.

ASPECTS OF HIDDEN AND INVISIBLE BELIEFS

★ A belief is hidden, invisible or transparent when one is living and operating through the belief without being consciously aware of it, or knowing about it. They're called invisible because one can't see them, and hidden because they operate subconsciously - below one's normal waking conscious awareness.

☆ Hidden and invisible beliefs may be helpful, as in the case of successful people who have trained themselves to "internalise" positive ones.

★ Negative invisible beliefs are self-sabotaging and most certainly not helpful, and can even be debilitating.

☆ These negative invisible beliefs have usually been adopted unknowingly, sometime in the past - most likely in childhood and adolescence.

★ When someone is choosing to **not** live consciously and deliberately, any hidden and invisible beliefs tend to automatically dominate and continue to influence their experiences.

KEY INSIGHTS

★ Hidden and invisible beliefs are characterised by these factors:

1 they tend to be totally and unquestionably true to the believer

2 they tend to be the beliefs you take for granted

3 the proof for holding a hidden or invisible belief is actually **produced** by the belief itself.

EXAMPLES OF HIDDEN AND INVISIBLE BELIEFS

"Beggars can't be choosers"

"Needs must when the devil drives"

"Well, that's the way life is"

"Dogs are always a nuisance"

"I can't do anything about ..."

"Happiness doesn't last"

"I'm no good with mechanical things"

"Doctors never know what's wrong with me"

"I am always busy because there is so much to do"

"It never rains, it pours"

"Chances are that ..."

"Life's a bitch, then you die"

"It never seems to work"

"I don't sleep well in strange and unfamiliar places"

"There is no hope for the world"

"You can't beat the system"

"There's no money around"

"It all depends upon ... (something else)"

"There are some crazy drivers on the roads"

"I can't get ahead no matter what I do"

"Cats like me"

"It's the rich that get richer and the poor that get the blame"

"It's beyond belief"

"The world is in a terrible mess"

"Being alive today is full of uncertainty"

EXERCISE FOR YOU TO DO

Exercise aims: to determine

1 the precise beliefs that create a particular situation you have in your life

2 the experiences (created by the belief) that reinforce the belief - which are the same experiences that create **certainty** in the belief.

Expected result: to gain relief from particular undesired situations, and to get closer to changing them for the better.

What to do

☆ This exercise is best done confidentially in pairs. You might enlist the help of a partner, counsellor or friend.

★ You can get the best results for yourself by being completely honest.

☆ Don't underestimate the simplicity, clarity and power of this exercise. The truth about your beliefs is often well camouflaged. Invisible beliefs become visible if you can spot them by allowing them to casually reveal themselves.

★ One person is the "client", while the other is a "counsellor", who guides and assists. You can swap over later if you want.

☆ The counsellor asks the questions and allows time for a clear understandable response, and moves from question 1 through to question 4. At this point, the counsellor moves from question 4 to question 5 and then back to 4 again, **until** the client gains an insight into the situation originally described.

★ The client usually experiences an "ah-ha!" sense of finding a belief that fits into or explains the described situation. Once he/she has gained a fresh view of the connection between something they **believe** and something they **experience,** the exercise is complete. It is then time to swap roles, if you want, or to choose another subject.

Questions

Write down your responses and/or other insights to these questions.

1   What would you like to change? Name a specific situation in your life.

2   What belief might someone have in order to experience this situation?

   For this question, you might suggest the "client" pictures someone else having this situation - it helps them to step back from the situation and take a wider view of it.

3   How would you prove this belief to be true? What evidence or proof is there?

4   What **other** belief might someone have in order to experience this situation?

5   How would you prove this belief to be true?

Now go back to question 4, and then move on to question 5 again **until the exercise feels complete**, or concludes with a new insight or understanding.

You'll probably end up discussing your findings at quite some length.

Come back to this exercise again if you want. More often than not, deeper insights will emerge, even from the same piece of ground that you've gone over before.

Belief Counselling Approaches

This chapter is intended to build on the exercise in the previous chapter.

It provides a framework for a "belief counsellor" to help a "client" to identify and change underlying and hidden important beliefs that cause and shape a client's life experiences.

IN SUMMARY

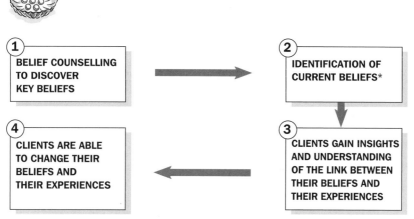

```
┌1─────────────────┐              ┌2─────────────────┐
│ BELIEF COUNSELLING│   ──────▶    │ IDENTIFICATION OF │
│ TO DISCOVER       │              │ CURRENT BELIEFS*  │
│ KEY BELIEFS       │              │                   │
└───────────────────┘              └───────────────────┘
                                            │
                                            ▼
┌4─────────────────┐              ┌3─────────────────┐
│ CLIENTS ARE ABLE  │              │ CLIENTS GAIN INSIGHTS│
│ TO CHANGE THEIR   │   ◀──────    │ AND UNDERSTANDING │
│ BELIEFS AND       │              │ OF THE LINK BETWEEN│
│ THEIR EXPERIENCES │              │ THEIR BELIEFS AND │
│                   │              │ THEIR EXPERIENCES │
└───────────────────┘              └───────────────────┘
```

* Sometimes it's enough to bring about or catalyse a change for the better, when a client just becomes aware of their actual and true beliefs.

BELIEF COUNSELLING - GUIDELINES

1   Find somewhere where you, a "counsellor", and a "client", will be undisturbed for a couple of hours.

2   Establish mutual confidentiality.

3   Use the belief counselling procedure below, remembering that clients may have been culturally conditioned to distort or misrepresent the truth about what they believe, and the objective facts about their experiences. The truth can sometimes be emotionally

uncomfortable, but it is always clarifying and liberating to "own up"!

4   The counsellor needs to be open to the validity of what the client is saying - but check it out!

5   Don't offer advice, explanations or belief solutions to the situations that clients present - aim for the discovery of the real beliefs first, and assist the client with this.

6   Every belief counselling session is unique, and a fresh open mind is needed. Expect the unexpected!

7   Be gently persistent, but move the client forward slowly through the procedure, taking notes if necessary, and respecting the client's viewpoint on all matters.

8   Your client will gain a new insight and understanding when you jointly reach a new perspective on the gap between what is believed and what is experienced.

     When these click and match, the important beliefs usually have feelings of **any** kind attached or associated with them, but the insight normally brings inspiration, clarity and a sense of "ah-ha! I see it now".

9   It's not necessarily the counsellor's job to try and make the client feel better; the counsellor's job is to serve the client's journey of discovery of the **causes** of his/her beliefs and experiences.

10   Belief counselling seeks to identify the causes of clients' situations. This is different from some therapeutic counselling procedures which might focus on alleviating clients' emotional feelings, rather than directly addressing and changing the original beliefs that created the situation in the first place.

11   These procedures take practice, some skill, some patience, some intuition, some awareness, and not everyone can do it successfully first time. But hopefully you'll find counselling with a belief perspective to be a very direct and useful technique.

12 Last, remember that unravelling some people's beliefs is like unravelling a ball of string. You have to start at one end and work gently inwards. Don't expect instant miracles: one counselling session alone might bring change, but five to ten sessions - or however many you feel are needed - are recommended over a period of time.

BELIEF COUNSELLING - PROCEDURES

First stage

1 Ask the client to describe the situation in their life that is either troubling them or creating problems. Get specific.

2 Ask simple direct questions to get a complete and clear picture in your mind about the situation presented.

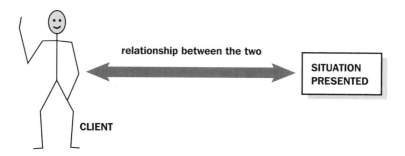

3 Establish the relationship between the client and the situation with factual and objective truth.

4 Look for

☆ what the client doesn't believe

★ what the client does believe

☆ conflicts between different things the client believes

★   putting aside what the client **wants** to believe

☆   putting aside what the client thinks they **should** believe

★   establishing from this, **how it actually is now** for the client, and how they feel about it.

5   Some further considerations:

☆   Are there any inconsistencies between different things the client is saying?

★   Is there a significant gap between what the client is experiencing and what he/she wants to experience? What beliefs explain the gap?

☆   What **behaviour** does the client engage in? Is this behaviour overcompensating for what they truly believe?

★   Has the client previously created a **similar** set of experiences and situations before (more than once)? Look for an underlying and established set of beliefs to explain these **patterns**.

☆   Note what the client doesn't say! Examine and question deliberate omissions so as to build a whole clear picture of what the client is experiencing.

★   Look for the underlying belief principles active behind overcompensating behaviours and motivations.

☆   Question all assumptions, and narrow matters down to specific items.

★   Sometimes clients don't tell the whole truth!

You as counsellor should now have a clear picture of the client and his/her situation.

Second stage

Your notebook may prove useful here.

1   With the situation clarified, the counsellor asks:

"What do you believe about the situation?"

Client answers: "..."

Question: "Why?"

Client answers: "Because ..."

Question: "And why is that so?"

Client answers: "Because ..."

Questions and answers are **repeated** until ...

2   An **underlying core belief, operating principle** or **state of being** emerges from the bottom of the pile of reasons.

3   A cause-and-effect relationship is established between a belief and evidence from the client that supports its existence.

4   Sometimes there are groups of self-supporting beliefs, but underneath there is usually one, maybe two, major beliefs holding the whole situation together.

WHAT IS BEING ACHIEVED?

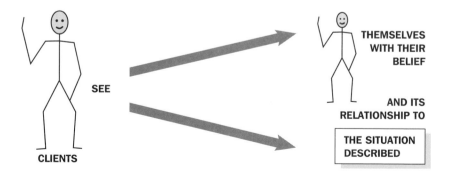

SEE

CLIENTS

THEMSELVES
WITH THEIR
BELIEF

AND ITS
RELATIONSHIP TO

THE SITUATION
DESCRIBED

THE AIM OF COUNSELLING

The counsellor is facilitating the client in stepping outside the way they are experiencing the situation described, and to view it from a belief-creation (cause-and-effect) perspective, so as to illuminate the way the client's actual core beliefs relate to their experiences.

The insights and understandings derived from this counselling procedure not only enable the client to change the determining belief, but also provide the basis for the client to change their behaviour and take different actions, which may prove more beneficial and effective.

SOME COMMON UNDERLYING CORE BELIEFS OR OPERATING PRINCIPLES

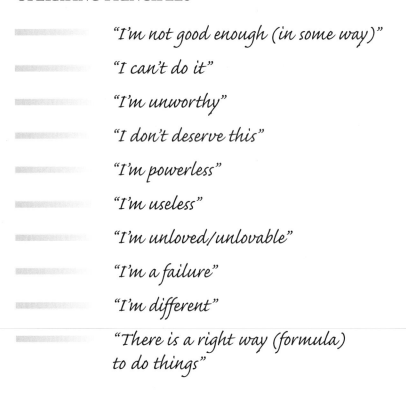

"I'm not good enough (in some way)"

"I can't do it"

"I'm unworthy"

"I don't deserve this"

"I'm powerless"

"I'm useless"

"I'm unloved/unlovable"

"I'm a failure"

"I'm different"

"There is a right way (formula) to do things"

"I can't trust myself"

"I'm right"

"I don't know how to"

"I'm bad"

"I'm just unlucky"

"I'm unhappy"

"There is nothing I can do"

"It's hopeless to try"

"Poor me"

"I'm a victim"

There are lots of others.

CHAPTER 4.6

BELIEFS, FEELINGS, VALUES AND ATTITUDES

From all the previous chapters, you now know that beliefs cause and create the experiences, events and circumstances you have in your life. So how do feelings and emotions affect this cause-and-effect relationship?

Feelings and emotions are activated and generated by **judgements** and **conditioning beliefs**, such as good and bad, right and wrong, that are placed parallel to, or on top of, the experiences. They automatically create the kind of emotional or feeling response a person has in any situation. Most of these conditioning beliefs are learned, and can be unlearned.

For example:

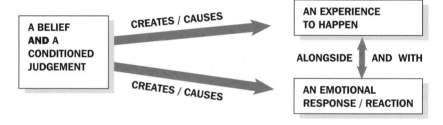

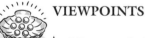 **VIEWPOINTS**

★ Most people feel something **as** or **after** something happens.

☆ Feelings and emotions can be determined by what is experienced, **and ...**

★ ... what is experienced is created from what is believed.

☆ Beliefs about feelings and emotions, their depth, strength, expression and importance, vary widely between men and women, young and old, and between cultural groups.

★ Emotions and feelings are influenced by personal beliefs about them.

☆ Emotions and feelings are generated by the judgements built into and alongside certain kinds of beliefs.

★ Emotions and feelings can become trapped behind walls of belief pretence (commonly protecting low self-esteem and "not-good-enough" types of core beliefs).

☆ Emotions and feelings can be manufactured by the imagination or influenced by reality or by both, as when a person watches an emotional film.

★ Emotions and feelings can be denied, shut down or shut off - resisted - usually to avoid pain and discomfort. These are normally wrapped up in new layers of disappointment and debilitating beliefs, so that the **true** emotions and feelings become completely hidden. **People have a tendency to move towards experiences that provide pleasure and away from those that cause them pain.**

☆ True emotions and feelings can become restored when one takes full responsibility for the authorship of what one is experiencing.

★ Emotional health is defined as much by the quality of emotional experience as by the freedom and flexibility of being able to move through emotional experiences without resistance.

MODES OF FUNCTIONING

People function in different ways and these modes are interchangeable, according to what state of being, or state of mind, they are in. Most people use one or sometimes two of the modes more often than the others.

Here are some modes:

Thinking - the mental, logical, cerebral mode.

Intuition - using knowingness, insight, ESP, sixth sense, hunches, dreams containing feelings and/or symbolism, etc.

Imagination - deliberate dreaming (can evoke and create levels of feeling).

Experiencing or being - feeling, sensing, emotional, a gut sense.

 ## EXERCISE FOR YOU TO DO

This is intended to explore the realm of emotions and feelings.

What emotions do you feel **most** of the time? Write down your self-assessment of the quality of your everyday feelings.

SOME OF THE
MOST COMMON EMOTIONS

These include

love

fear

anger

depression

resentment

jealousy

envy

hatred

guilt

rage

All these are caused, influenced and activated by the type of beliefs you hold. By the time any of these emotions are felt and experienced, the original beliefs responsible for their presence have already created something. Therefore, almost all negative emotions are indirectly caused by a form of unawareness or powerlessness, plus an inability to create the kinds of experiences desired.

HEALTHY EMOTIONAL ORIENTATIONS

In general, there are four main healthy emotional orientations:

1   being willing to experience your true feelings rather than resist, deny or suppress them

2   having positive attitudes

3   having gratitude and appreciation for all that you are, all that you have, and all that you experience **now**, this moment onwards, no matter how life is

4   having the willingness to practise unconditional forgiveness and, particularly, self-forgiveness, in all matters.

For-give-ness means to let go of **any** emotional blame or attachment to any past circumstances or events that continue to cloud the enjoyment of what is happening now (in the present time) in your life.

Forgiveness doesn't mean you necessarily condone other people's past actions - it just means you are now willing to let go or release what you may be holding onto emotionally.

Forgiveness can release the cause and blocked emotional energy of any past blames, hurts, regrets, disappointments and guilts, and can therefore enable the restoration of greater creative power and quality of experience.

Self-forgiveness means releasing yourself from all self-judgements for all personal actions, inactions, mistakes, failures, choices and decisions that emotionally still have repercussions for you today.

Forgiveness has its own magic, and comes about naturally simply through the attitude of heart - of being **willing** to forgive.

It is important that self-forgiveness is used to release a person from self-hatred, self-criticism and self-judgement which tend to be some of the main causes of personal failure and disappointment in life.

 EXERCISE FOR YOU TO DO

List all the things that you are truly grateful for in your life now.

List all the people and the things that you are now willing to unconditionally forgive them for.

Repeat these to yourself every day for a month.

List all the self-judgements, self-criticisms and self-blames you hold against yourself about past experiences that you are now willing to unconditionally forgive yourself for.

Reviewing this exercise

Put a date in your diary or journal, or make a note somewhere, to look at this exercise a month from today. **Please don't skip this!**

After a month, did you notice feeling better about yourself and your life?

Listening to your inner voice and feelings is important, because what that voice and those feelings say and communicate to you can reveal insights, conditions and beliefs.

It is the beliefs that contain and cause feelings that are the significant ones, and are the ones more likely to be deeply held. Thoughts, feelings and beliefs can be perceived through **any** sensory channel of awareness, including body sensations or knowing something (but you don't know how).

Jot down some examples of your intuition or hunches that proved right.

Suppressed, hidden or unexpressed feelings and emotional energies can become trapped in your being, tending to create dis-ease or illness. The continuous habit of avoiding or ignoring your true feelings can lead to feelings of numbness or depression.

 EXERCISE FOR YOU TO DO

Exercise aim: to restore feeling what you are truly feeling.

Choose a time when you are feeling strongly about something. Sit down, close your eyes, and relax. Connect your breathing and allow it to settle into a rhythm. Allow yourself to fully feel exactly what you are feeling, without judgement or taking action. Continue until the feeling changes and your mood moves on and you feel more centred and still inside yourself.

Remind yourself - that **whatever** you are feeling, it is all right to feel like this.

So what did your feelings tell you?

So what can you resolve to do to alleviate or change this situation for the better?

If it feels right, resolve to take action on this.

VALUES

Everyone has their own personal and internal set of values. These are made up of what you value and don't value. They can include

★ moral values

☆ spiritual values

★ personal values

☆ codes of ethics and behaviour

★ religious creeds.

EXERCISE FOR YOU TO DO

Take a while to consider what
your values are.

CHAPTER 4.7

Aliveness and Well-Being Beliefs

From an early age, we are all exposed to cultural beliefs about life and death. The mind and emotions can directly affect the health and performance of the body, and any hidden or unspoken beliefs about the limitations imposed on us by ageing, or the inevitability or unpredictability of death, can affect what happens to us now.

But if it's true that we can take responsibility for our lives and can create the experiences and circumstances we want, doesn't this mean we should have at least **some** influence over the length and quality of our lives?

If a person's beliefs and desires weigh more heavily in favour of death rather than being alive, it may be more difficult for them to live a rich and full life, than to age, get sick and die. "Life", goes the saying, "is what you want it to be".

 EXERCISE FOR YOU TO DO

Take some time to yourself to contemplate some of the broader questions of existence.

My reasons for wanting to live are ...

My reasons for not wanting to live (if any) are ...

My reasons about being able to experience living fully are ...

My beliefs about death and dying are ...

 VIEWPOINT

As will be discussed in Chapter 4.9, "Genetic, cultural and group beliefs", human and animal genes contain molecular codes and behavioural belief and instinct patterns, stored at a cellular level. Our health and well-being are maintained by these instructions buried within the cells.

These instructions, or codes, regulate the creation of new cells and the destruction of old ones. Both functions are essential for maintaining body health and balance. But when this balance becomes severely distorted by physical, emotional or biochemical stress, ageing and death are accelerated.

It is possible that certain beliefs can reduce overall stress levels, and even avert ageing. Some people even propose that these beliefs may actually remove it, because lower stress levels can slow down the ageing process. A theoretical computer model once estimated by calculation that, given **perfect** conditions and no stress, the human body has the capacity to live for 250,000 years!

This possibility is almost too fantastic to be true, but we can read about mystical and spiritual traditions of immortality going back through history to the ancient sages and the Greek gods; and through to many fictional writings about immortality, such as Henry Rider Haggard's "She" (1887). The Bible also mentions people living for hundreds of years, and characters like Dracula occasionally pop up in fiction as immortals!

We just don't know whether future centuries may uncover the secrets of immortality, or even of how to live a very long time. Yet, today, there are so many cultural beliefs that deny or ignore this uncharted frontier of human experience. The situation seems analogous to the sheer weight of disbelief in times past, when people just laughed at the idea of humans walking on the Moon.

Nevertheless, the possibility of immortality does at least exist. Nature itself provides one example of how ageing can be reversed: several scientific studies have demonstrated that old honey-bee workers fed a special diet become young again!

The immortalist, living-forever philosophy can be summarised as:

*"You can live as long as you want to
and want to as long as you live."*

The future can contain great unimagined possibilities!

SHORT-TERM AND LONG-TERM BELIEFS

In this chapter we'll take a fairly quick look at beliefs around the short-term and long-term future. As discussed in the previous chapter, healthy positive belief expectations can influence future outcomes and events.

Yet we live in an unsure world. Life, and nature, are uncertain! **Nothing** in this universe is assured, and no one actually **knows** for sure about any other universe, or any other existence anywhere else! But that's the deal Existence hands us when we are born. Faced with the truth of that immensity, and the immensity of that truth, it's not surprising some sensitive people feel a little overwhelmed ...

 EXERCISE FOR YOU TO DO

Take some time for contemplation.

My beliefs about the uncertainty of the future are ...

 VIEWPOINTS

A well-balanced life requires **both** short-term and long-term beliefs and expectations. If a person has a majority of operating beliefs that are active and focused upon **only** the immediate future it may mean that their life is dominated by some of these:

☆ *uncertainty*

★ *struggle*

☆ *poverty*

★ *survival*

☆ *crisis management*

★ *getting by and muddling through*

☆ *success or failure - everything being at stake.*

Whereas, a person who has clear and definite long-term beliefs and expectations has the benefit of these influencing and clarifying short-term beliefs and situations. Long-term beliefs and expectations tend to create

★ *certainty*   ☆ *stability*

☆ *fulfilment*   ★ *well-being.*

★ *security*

EXERCISE FOR YOU TO DO

This is intended to refer primarily to your beliefs concerning yourself. As our destinies are inevitably bound up with the destiny of certain things outside our immediate sphere of influence, you might want to think also about how your beliefs about the future are connected to factors such as

☆ other people close to you - friends and family

★ other people more distant - employers, colleagues, the local community

☆ the future of the nation

★ the world at large.

My beliefs about the short-term future are:

My beliefs about the long-term future are:

For more on choosing short-term and long-term goals, see Section 5, "New possibilities - creating your future".

CHAPTER 4.9

GENETIC, CULTURAL AND GROUP BELIEFS

Let's move on from the final exercise you may have already done at the end of the previous chapter.

"No man is an island", goes the saying. We cannot exist in total isolation, and our thoughts and beliefs just cannot help being influenced by our origins and our environment

☆   as a species with biological and instinctual patterns of behaviour, and

★   as part of our culture.

GENETIC BELIEFS

The long-standing debate amongst psychologists about Nature (genetics and inherited attributes) versus Nurture (conditioning and social environment) is still continuing, and will probably never be completely settled.

Which affects us more? Evidence flies back and forth, but common sense suggests that neither constitutes the sole truth: it seems obvious that both play a part.

For an example of evidence on the Nature side, recent scientific studies of identical twins and their long-term behaviour patterns have indicated the greater significance of genetic predetermination. They have also indicated how identical twins' preprogrammed beliefs affect their behaviour.

 NOTE

All the different races in the world only vary by about 0.5% in their genetic similarities!

But whatever, there is a third factor in the debate, which seems to be mostly ignored. That is, mature adults can exercise their individualistic free choice and self-determination. We can choose to behave exactly how we want to, starting now, no matter what bases Nature and Nurture have initially provided us with.

 VIEWPOINT

Adult human behaviour is influenced by a mixture of all the **three** factors illustrated in this diagram.

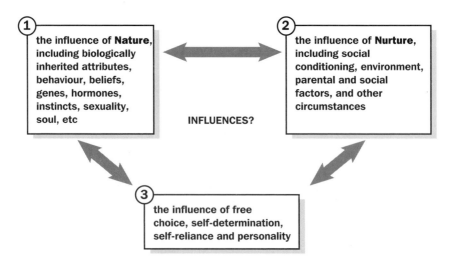

① the influence of Nature, including biologically inherited attributes, behaviour, beliefs, genes, hormones, instincts, sexuality, soul, etc

INFLUENCES?

② the influence of Nurture, including social conditioning, environment, parental and social factors, and other circumstances

③ the influence of free choice, self-determination, self-reliance and personality

WHAT FACTORS INFLUENCE HUMAN BEHAVIOUR AND QUALITY OF LIFE?

Let's look at two. They are

☆ cultural beliefs

★ group beliefs.

1 Cultural beliefs

Some major examples of the influence of cultural beliefs occur in the realms of:

★ *fashion*

☆ *arts*

★ *leisure*

☆ *sport*

★ *music*

☆ *literature*

★ *historical culture*

☆ *geographical or regional influences*

☆ *language*

★ *the media*

☆ *social conditioning and education*

★ *social welfare and civil rights*

☆ *technology and science*

★ *other personal interests and pursuits.*

Most cultural beliefs are shared by small or large groups of people, and are also, by definition, group beliefs.

EXERCISE FOR YOU TO DO

Write down two things you believe about ...

1 fashion

2 the arts

3 leisure

4 sport

5 music

6 literature

7 your historical culture

8 geographical or regional influences

9	language	11	social conditioning and education	13	other personal interests and pursuits
10	the media	12	social welfare and civil rights	14	technology and science

2 Group beliefs

Group, shared or collective common beliefs have a tremendous impact on the world. Collective beliefs have shaped history - common assumptions about morality, politics, religions, human rights and the ways we behave towards each other.

Some common examples of major group beliefs involve:

☆   religions, cults and sects

★   political ideologies, politics and the law

☆   nationality and race

★   money, economics and business

☆   the future of humankind and the world.

At the centre of group, shared or collective beliefs remains the most important belief element: **self-interest.**

 EXERCISE FOR YOU TO DO

Just for the sake of curiosity and insight, when you are watching the News, or reading the newspaper, notice how shared beliefs amongst different population groups lie at the root of so much human activity. Collective beliefs have immense power to determine our collective destiny.

ALLOWANCES AND OTHER BELIEFS

It's part of the human condition that we can never know all there is to know. There will always be more mystery than illumination, and we will forever be incomplete. So we'll just have to make allowances for ourselves!

This incompleteness also extends into the realms of thought and belief.

SOME REASONS AND ALLOWANCES WHY THE CONCEPT OF BELIEFS CAN NEVER BE COMPLETE

☆ There can never be any full understanding of what life is.

★ Things are created and happen in their own time.

☆ Understanding the theory of beliefs is not the same as living and experiencing them.

★ A belief is valueless unless you test it and live by it.

☆ Sometimes explanations cannot account for what there is, or what is experienced.

★ Life always has some magic and mystery.

☆ Truth and experience are relative to each individual.

There are lots of others.

SOME THINGS THAT CANNOT BE EXPLAINED

Creation is full of unexplained natural mysteries - so many, it's not possible to list them all. Here are some to muse over at your leisure.

★ *birth deformities, reincarnation, life after death*

☆ *the natural miracles of life that happen around you all the time!*

★ *astrology, destiny, fate and fortune*

☆ *other worlds, other dimensions, other beings*

★ *infinity and parallel universes*

★ *god and the origin of life*

☆ *any mysterious or extraordinary event (life can be stranger than fiction)*

★ *chaos theory*

☆ *the presence of time, matter and energy*

★ *there are always unknown factors or "grey areas" in creating and in life.*

 EXERCISE FOR YOU TO DO

Take some time to contemplate each of the above mysteries and phenomena individually.

OTHER TOPICS NOT COVERED

☆ *accidents and disasters*

★ *prophecies*

☆ *inevitability*

★ *fame and adoration*

☆ *suffering*

★ *predictability*

☆ *dependency*

★ *control*

☆ *surrender*

★ *class, social status and respectability*

☆ *humour*

★ *adversity*

☆ *risk*

★ *vulnerability*

☆ *safety*

★ *beliefs about beliefs*

☆ *luck and chance*

★ *community*

SECTION 5
NEW POSSIBILITIES - CREATING YOUR FUTURE

5.1 CHOOSING YOUR OWN GOALS AND DREAMS
5.2 ALIGNING YOUR GOALS AND BELIEFS
5.3 SIMPLE TECHNIQUES TO ASSIST YOU IN CREATING WHAT YOU WANT

"What is now proved was once only imagined."

William Blake (1757 - 1827)
British poet, painter and engraver.

"Nothing great was ever achieved without enthusiasm."

Ralph Waldo Emerson (1803 - 1882)

"A wise man will make more opportunities than he finds."

Francis Bacon (1561 - 1626)
English philosopher who put forward the idea of scientific knowledge based on experimentation and observation - commonly known as the inductive method.

*I can
choose
my future
path in life.*

CHOOSING YOUR OWN GOALS AND DREAMS

It is good to honour your healthy desires by having goals and dreams of some kind that are personally suited to you. To be in personal alignment means to be in agreement with, **and** to work towards, having some goal or goals. Personal misalignment comes from having uncertain, conflicting or non-existent goals.

People who have no goal or direction are in danger of becoming confused, erratic and bogged down in trivia or problems. Having goals creates specific mental focus and allows the subconscious mental workings to get active.

Put simply, having a vision, goal or goals not only gives the mind something to get on with, but also allows for the natural harnessing of the forces of change to work in your favour.

It is important to choose goals that are perfect for you - PFY - rather than having just any old goal. You can do this by reasoning and balancing appropriate goals, formulated with your intellect and with your intuitive feelings:

☆ thinking that the goal is reasonable - you think you can achieve it, and

★ it feels right for you.

And what's more ...

☆ **if you don't request something with thoughts, visions or prayers, how do you expect to have it or experience it?**

You'll know when a PFY goal is right for you, because you'll very likely feel enthusiastic, excited and uplifted with energy when you contemplate it.

A non-perfect-for-you (non-PFY) goal, on the other hand, is usually something you feel you "have to do", which might feel like an irksome task, and can be difficult, frustrating, gruelling. Generally, it is going to create lots of stress for you.

So, it is valuable to know the difference between these two types of goals, and

1   to choose goals that are realistic in relation to your life now; they needn't be wildly huge goals at first, because failure would just lead to disappointment

2   to set simple, small and achievable goals initially and gradually increase their size, scope and content as you come to establish a successful pattern of goal achievement.

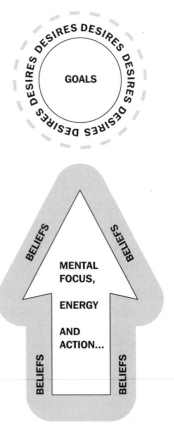

The best goals to choose now are those sitting just on the edge or outer limits of what you believe is possible.

PROBLEMS WITH GOALS AND DREAMS

1   Many people don't really know what they want as a dream or a major life goal. For people like these, it's best to start with small

objectives and plans first, and then allow larger goals when a pattern of success with these smaller projects and desires is established.

2 Many people who don't seem to achieve life-long goals, dreams and desires often come up with excuses like "I can't do it because ...".

Such excuses commonly include things like

★ blame

☆ procrastination

★ justification

... which people often indulge in, **instead** of getting involved in some form of **action**.

3 When important goals and dreams are not realised over a period of time, they tend to become negative. Many important goals and dreams are frequently hidden and buried underneath personal failures.

4 Many of the solutions to the "problems" of non-goal achievement are often disguised and held within the problems themselves.

5 Important goals and dreams have to have a challenge element within them - otherwise you don't get the chance to experience any worthwhile satisfaction upon achieving or attaining them.

6 Money is not the answer. **Most** worthwhile goals require dedication, enthusiasm, energy and action at the outset.

EXERCISE FOR YOU TO DO

Exercise aim: to determine your true life goals and to provide a clear life plan. (You may already be engaged in some of these activities using other books and studies.)

Take lots of time to consider and contemplate these questions, and jot down your answers. **Think big!**

1   What would you be doing today if you had all the money you wanted?

2   What you do want to achieve in the next year?

3   What do you want to own by the end of next year?

4   What would you like to do by the end of next year?

5   What excites you the most?

6   What would you have to **become** to do what you want?

7   Where would you like to be in two years' time?

8   Where would you like to be in five years' time?

9   Where would you like to be in ten years' time?

10 What goals have you given up on?

11 What would you **really** like to do?

12 If you knew you just couldn't fail, what would you do?

13 When are you happiest?

14 What do people whom you admire do?

15 What were your goals when you were younger?

16 What would you like to do, just for the heck of it?

17 What do you consider that it's too late to start on?

18 If it weren't for ... (fill in), what would you do?

19 What might not be impossible?

You'll probably enjoy coming back to this exercise time and time again. It's inevitable that what you might think about today, and write down, might not be the same as what you contemplate tomorrow or next week. Revising your goals and responses often will give you clarity and insight.

Besides, what is true today might be rubbish tomorrow ... and what you might think of as rubbish today might just turn out to be the break you've been looking for. Seeing things in a new light from day to day can often reveal many hidden truths and potentials.

ASSESSING YOUR POTENTIAL GOALS

It is suggested you make a list of all your major goals.

Draw a table like this:

		SCORES FROM THE 7 QUESTIONS	TOTAL SCORE
1	*To become debt-free within 12 months*	5+7+8+6+10+7+8	51
2			
3			
4			

Down the left, write out a list of all your major goals.

Next, consider each goal individually.

Answer **all** of the following questions, allocating points from 1 to 10, where

1 represents "very doubtful", and
10 represents "very certain"

to **each goal**, and write them all in the column under "Scores from the seven questions".

Questions

1   Does your goal invite interest and attention? Does thinking about it

increase your interest?

2   Does the pursuit of this goal produce something of real personal value to you?

3   Does the goal offer benefits to other people **equal** to your own?

4   Does the goal represent an opportunity for more self-development (for example, better knowledge, understanding, competence, responsibility etc)?

5   Is the goal possibly in general agreement and alignment with the wider goals of other people and with broader goals of humankind (for example, world or environmental welfare)?

6   Does the goal allow more personal creativity and some degree of self-management?

7   Does the goal allow the opportunity to receive admiration from others and for personal recognition?

Now add up all seven scores for each goal, and write the totals in the column under "Total score".

You can now evaluate and compare your goals. It should be clear how important, or not, they are.

If you scored:

☆   0 - 30 points ... you might consider totally rethinking this goal

★   31 - 50 points ... you might like to modify and adjust this goal

☆   51 - 70 points ... this goal is perfect for you.

Next, take a while to imagine an even bigger and more expansive goal that incorporates all of your goals together. Write it down.

How does this make you feel?

EXERCISE FOR YOU TO DO

Exercise aim: to have another look at what you'd like your future to be like.

Jot down some answers to these questions.

1   What do you want to do?

2   What do you want to be?

3   What do you want to have?

4   What do you want to give to others?

In the light of just having done the exercise before this one, do you notice any difference from any other similar notes on evaluating goals that you may have made in the past?

How does this make you feel?

SOME ADDITIONAL NOTES ABOUT GOALS

1   Don't force or enrol other people to be part of your goals and dreams, unless you have their willing consent and cooperation.

2   Only share your goals with the kind of people who would support and believe in your success.

3   Don't assume that other people will automatically be enthusiastic and in favour of your goals and dreams - particularly if they are not doing the same. Keep your goals and dreams selectively private.

4   Avoid those people who tend to openly criticise your endeavours, pour cold water on your dreams with their limited thinking and negativity, and generally try to dishearten you!

5   If you are not specific and sure about what you really want - why expect to achieve or have anything at all?

6   Check that you do not have mutually exclusive or conflicting goals - ones that cannot exist together at the same time. If this is the case, give priority to those goals that appeal more on an emotional or feeling basis and are in alignment with what you value more in your heart.

7   The only things between you and what you want are your beliefs and your actions.

ALIGNING YOUR GOALS AND BELIEFS

The exercises in the previous chapter contained some quite searching and demanding self-examination. Congratulate yourself.

Now that you have written down some goals and dreams that you want, you'll find it beneficial and enjoyable to

1   think of them regularly and keep them alive and active in your mind

2   review and reassess them

3   reset new goals as others are completed

4   persevere and be persistent with your goals - this great quality can outlast all failures, disappointments and disillusionments

5   check that your beliefs are in alignment with your goals, as misaligned or conflicting beliefs are frequently the cause of unfulfilled goals and dreams ...

Beliefs either carry you towards your goals, or they keep you away from them.

For example, a person might think:

"I want to be a rock star."

but actually, believe that:

"Success is a pipe-dream, I'll never learn to play guitar, and anyway, I'm just one of millions of past-it wannabees."

6   ensure that your goals and dreams are not allowed to fade and be misplaced at the expense of other everyday matters

7   know where you are in relation to achieving your goals and dreams.

EXERCISE FOR YOU TO DO

Exercise aim: to realign your attention and energy with your goals and dreams.

Expected result: to create a clearer and easier path to successful goal achievement and dream fulfilment.

1   Make a list of all your current key goals. There may lots of them, or only a few, but list them all anyway.

2   Make a list of all your major weekly current activities.

Now add a + (plus), or a - (minus), to denote whether these activities help or hinder your key goals.

Now for some more things to write down ...

1   What percentage (roughly) of your weekly time goes towards your goals?

2   Make a list of all your major monthly expenses.

3   What percentage (roughly) of your monthly expenses goes towards your goals?

4   Divide your journal page into two columns with headings like this:

KEY GOALS	BELIEFS I HAVE ABOUT THEM
1	1
	2
	3
2	4

On the left, write all your key goals.
On the right, make a list of any beliefs you have about **each** key goal you have. Keep going until you have no more!

Now add a + (plus), or a - (minus) to **each** belief to denote whether that belief is either a help or a hindrance to the fulfilment of that goal.

Next, rewrite any hindering (negative or limited) beliefs you may have into positive ones that you want.

Come back to this as often as new thoughts occur to you.

5   This next item is an opportunity for you to check out how strong your belief actually is in achieving each of your goals.

Write each key goal again, and allocate a percentage score from 0% to 100% to quantify your certainty that you will achieve this particular goal. Use headings like this:

GOAL	PERCENTAGE OF CERTAINTY IN GOAL ACHIEVEMENT
1	%
2	%

NOTE

If you lack faith, and carry doubts about achieving your goals, you are self-sabotaging all your efforts so far. You will be in danger of severely diminishing or limiting your valuable certainty in believing you'll get what you want.

But if you believe in the strong certainty that you will achieve your goals and dreams, even though there is no evidence of how, why or when it could happen, you open the magic of life that makes these things happen for real. It's all about believing openly and unconditionally, without any doubts.

CHAPTER 5.3

SIMPLE TECHNIQUES TO ASSIST YOU IN CREATING WHAT YOU WANT

This is a very important and practical chapter, and you are quite likely to very much enjoy the techniques it offers.

It is a fundamental, crucial and invaluable gift you give yourself when you truly understand the usefulness and significance of aligning and harnessing the creative power of your subconscious mind to create what you want.

As mentioned already many times in previous chapters, most beliefs, abilities, talents, memories and knowledge are all stored and accessed from below the conscious level in our minds.

This subconscious mind possesses the most fascinating and incredible functions and mechanisms, which even modern science only partially understands. Yet, even though scientific and theoretical knowledge of the human brain is far from complete, it does not detract from the fact that you **know**, and you can observe, that your subconscious works very well!

FUNCTIONS OF THE SUBCONSCIOUS MIND

Some of the most important ones are

★   maintaining overall bodily health

☆   heartbeat, breathing and metabolism (autonomic nervous system)

★   the ability to filter and interpret all sensory experiences such as sound, sight, feel, smell, imagination **and** intuition

☆ the access and recall of memory

★ the assimilation of any skill, ability or talent

☆ the ability to learn

★ the assimilation of all knowledge, language and meaning

☆ **the storage of all current beliefs in present time.**

There are others, of course. But the list shows that our lives are almost entirely governed and regulated by what happens at the subconscious level in the human mind or brain.

 VIEWPOINT

In general ...

★ the conscious mind has the power to consciously rationalise, think, decide and direct the subconscious mind

☆ the subconscious mind holds the power of belief and creativity.

The relationship between the conscious and the subconscious minds is a bit like that between a car and its driver. The driver, representing the conscious mind, decides on the overall direction, steering and speed of the car. The driver gives the car instructions, through the controls, and the car responds exactly and precisely.

The car, representing the subconscious mind, is the vehicle. It possesses attributes of power and performance, which it makes available to the driver according to instructions.

Both car and driver need each other for them to go anywhere.

The subconscious mind will respond exactly and precisely to whatever instructions you give it. It has the power to take your outer life exactly and precisely where you instruct it.

NOTE

☆   The most important and valuable thing in this book is about learning how to direct and use the unlimited power of your subconscious mind.

Dwell on this:

THE UNLIMITED POWER OF YOUR SUBCONSCIOUS MIND!

Enjoy letting the full meaning of this phrase sink in. Contemplate it often, repeating it to yourself anywhere, anytime.

Unlimited - means just that.

Your subconscious - means yours.

CREATIVE ATTRIBUTES OF THE SUBCONSCIOUS MIND

1   The subconscious mind holds and creates your experiences consistently with the beliefs stored in it, held in past and present time.

2   The subconscious mind requires **specific and repeated** instructions for it to know what to do.

3   The subconscious cannot rationalise and decide things by itself. For you to create anything new and useful, your subconscious and

conscious minds need to work together cooperatively.

4   The subconscious mind cannot distinguish the difference between reality (what it real) and imagined reality (what is suggested to be real) unless instructed; and therefore, it is impressionable by the **power of suggestion** and direction.

5   The subconscious mind can be an unlimited source of ideas, inspiration, insights and solutions.

6   The subconscious mind has the ability to adjust space, time and matter to complete your goals.

7   The subconscious mind is a two-way mechanism. It can receive instructions to create **and** provide answers.

USING YOUR SUBCONSCIOUS MIND TO ASSIST YOU IN CREATING YOUR GOALS

First, select specific goals you want to achieve, or experiences you want to create. Then you can apply the creative power of your subconscious mind to help you manifest or create them.

Now choose your five most important goals and make an imagined picture or visualisation about them, to include

1   clear details about exactly how you want your goal to be

2   yourself being within, or next to, the goal; only include other people who want to be included

3   the imagined sights, sounds, smells and the feel of the goal

4   the goal completed as an end result

5   the timescale by which time the goal is completed

6   the feelings you want to experience on completing your goal.

Write down your five most important goals.

HOW TO VISUALISE YOUR GOALS

1   The subconscious mind is most accessible and impressionable before and after times of activity, and during times of deep relaxation.

2   Find a few minutes every day for regular visualisation. Get comfortable and close your eyes. Imagine your goals being completed - repeated focus and attention directs the subconscious mind most effectively.

3   Practise using goal visualisation daily.

4   See the goal completed and allow yourself to contemplate in detail all the different aspects of your goal. Indulge yourself in imagining your goal as **already** completed.

5   Take all the usual required action to bring your goals into being in the real world.

KEY INSIGHTS

☆   Keep holding your visualisations and visions - but let things happen naturally!

★   There is always a time delay in creating your goal - be patient!

☆   When your goals and beliefs are in alignment, life unfolds and things happen at the right time!

SECTION 6
THEMES TO CONSIDER

6.1   HAPPINESS AND FULFILMENT
6.2   LOVE AND RELATIONSHIPS
6.3   MONEY, WORK AND CAREER
6.4   WELFARE, HEALTH AND ENVIRONMENT

"What you need is the will to believe. You don't have to pursue happiness - it is there. You become what you believe."

Anthony Hopkins
British actor.

"If your wife and children leave you, your business goes bust and the neighbours are taking potshots at you - why be miserable as well?"

Lionel Fifield
Australian self-improvement expert.

"My secret to long life and happiness is doing what I enjoy. My doctor advised me that 14 cigars a day and three Martinis isn't good for me at my age - but he's dead now!"

George Burns (1896 - 1996!)
American entertainer and comic, who accomplished his goal of celebrating his 100th birthday!

I can create
joy, fulfilment
and well-being
in my life as
I choose.

CHAPTER 6.1

HAPPINESS AND FULFILMENT

The ideas that life is just about acquiring possessions, or even surrendering to your desires, can both lead to disappointment. There is no specific formula which can guarantee anyone love, joy, happiness and fulfilment in their lives.

But there are certain factors which can dramatically increase the chances of finding it. Successful people invariably

1   have high self-esteem

2   have control over the general direction of their life

3   have the freedom and ability to choose to do those activities which naturally bring them pleasure and enjoyment - whatever they might be

4   have beliefs that create quality experiences and support their well-being - their values and beliefs are in alignment with the qualities of their goals; they get fulfilment and satisfaction from fully realising their personal aims or potential

5   have **realistic** and defined goals

6   have a tendency to focus mostly on the good news and the good things in life

7   are usually good at achieving the tasks they set themselves

8   have an ability to enjoy themselves and their lives - no matter what!

After all, that is what life is for! ... very happy people are often viewed suspiciously by others who might suspect that there is something wrong with them!

9   honour their own tastes about what makes them happy

10   believe that they and their lives are worthwhile.

EXERCISE FOR YOU TO DO

Exercise aim: to put yourself in the shoes of a successful person - just to find out what it feels like.

Imagine you are now a successful person with all the attributes and qualities described in the list above.

Write everything you feel and think about having these qualities, as if you had them now.

KEY INSIGHT

★   You can allow yourself to be happy - for no reason at all! Happiness is not something you have to earn, deserve, work for or pay for. Happiness and fulfilment naturally come from the inside of your being when there is an absence of resistance or negativity ... this is why in the long term it is difficult to sustain a source of happiness if it depends only on someone or something outside of yourself.

Surprisingly, people do have negative beliefs towards happiness. Many people fear that

☆   it won't last

★   it is silly

☆   being happy is too self-indulgent

★   they would feel guilty about being happy - "just look at the problems in the world"

☆   it might mean their life or themselves would have to change in some way.

Not only that, they might be frightened to take specific steps towards increasing the level of happiness they experience.

Some people have **conditions** attached to achieving happiness and fulfilment:

*"I'll be happy **when** I win the lottery"*

*"I'll be happy **after** I get divorced again"*

*"I'll be happy **if** someone loves me properly"*

... and so on.

All these conditional beliefs prevent people from experiencing happiness and enjoyment by placing the prospective arrival of happiness constantly somewhere in the future. Why not look for happiness in the same place you may have lost it?

Likewise, there is a similar false assumption, that some people maintain, that certain events or things have to occur **before** life can change for the better.

EXERCISE FOR YOU TO DO

Does that last phrase you've just read apply to you? Jot down a few thoughts on the reasons why you believe you can't be happy now.

EVIDENCE

Scientific evidence shows that you can deliberately increase and develop your ability to be happy by smiling and focusing on enjoyment. Happiness is excellent for your overall health, your muscles, hormones and brainwaves!

MORE RESISTANCE TO HAPPINESS

Some people **fear** what would happen to them if they are

★ happier

☆   different

★   more powerful, assertive and in control of their lives

☆   more like who they want to be.

 EXERCISE FOR YOU TO DO

Exercise aim: to identify your fears and resistances.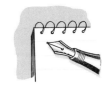

Write down your fears about being really happy.

It's as well not to ignore them or brush them aside. If you don't pinpoint them they will continue to rule the roost, and will continue to undermine your progress towards well-being.

 IN SUMMARY

The responsibility for your own happiness is in your own hands, and in your own heart!

LOVE AND RELATIONSHIPS

A vast literature exists on these topics, and this is a huge and potentially involved theme.

There is plenty of other material in the bookshops for you to browse, but here are a few viewpoints.

 VIEWPOINTS

☆ *Men and women are different, but can be treated equally and fairly.*

★ *A person's relationships with other people are only as good as their beliefs and their self-esteem.*

☆ *Love can be experienced, but not explained.*

★ *Love is simple and is the most natural of all emotions.*

☆ *Relationships with other people can bring the greatest joys, and the greatest sorrows.*

★ *Love is experienced by aligning one's beliefs with the values and feelings one feels in one's heart.*

☆ *Greater amounts of love can be experienced by releasing the barriers to it.*

★ *Unconditional love is the most powerful and pure form of love, as it carries no conditions or expectations.*

EXERCISE FOR YOU TO DO

Time now for more reflection.

Make notes about your current experiences of your relationships with other people.

What are your best relationship experiences?

What are your worst?

Write down your greatest grievances about what other people didn't do for you, or did against you in the past.

Write down: "I am willing to unconditionally forgive ... for ..."

Repeat this until you have no more negative feelings towards those people.

Then write: "I am loved by other people because ..."

And: "I am not loved by other people because ..."

And: "Other people like me because ..."

 VIEWPOINT

Love can be the key to be willing to create enough openness or room in which something is allowed to change.

MONEY, WORK AND CAREER

*"The only place where success comes before work
is in a dictionary."*
Vidal Sassoon

"Genius begins great works; labour alone finishes them."
Joseph Joubert

Money is an exchange medium based on, and representing, value and energy. Money is also a language, understood by virtually everyone in the world, and its influence is far greater than any religion.

The most important single factor in making and attracting money is self-esteem. However:

★   if you believe in the power of money - you'll notice what it can do in the world and what its absence can mean

☆   if you believe in your lack of money - you'll probably create debts

★   if you believe in your ability to make money - you'll probably never have any financial problems at all.

IN SUMMARY

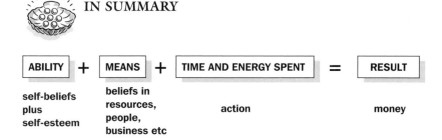

ABILITY	+	MEANS	+	TIME AND ENERGY SPENT	=	RESULT
self-beliefs plus self-esteem		beliefs in resources, people, business etc		action		money

The beliefs in money that businesspeople have, including the level of confidence in business markets, determine how stock markets, foreign exchanges and commodity markets behave.

EXERCISE FOR YOU TO DO

1 Write down all your positive associations to money. (What does it represent to you?)

2 Write down all your negative associations to money.

3 What is your usual experience of money? What do you believe about it?

4 Write down your mother's view of money.

5 Write down your father's view of money.

6 Write down your family's view of money.

7 Write down what you want to believe and experience about money.

8 What are your experiences and beliefs about work?

9 Have you recently worked hard for money or struggled to survive? What beliefs do you have that create the circumstances you experience?

SOME COMMON BELIEFS ABOUT MONEY

"You have to compete to survive in today's world"

"You have to make money"

"You have to work hard to succeed at anything"

or the usual one ...

"I can't afford it"

This last one can be an especially limiting and damaging belief to have, because it can continually create and assume an anticipated present and future inability to afford something.

Whereas both these beliefs ...

"I am going to afford it soon"

"I choose not to afford it now"

... are more flexible and open to increasing prosperity and changing spending patterns that the "I can't afford it" type of belief.

 KEY INSIGHT

★ It is common to believe that money can solve all your problems and automatically provide the experiences you desire. However, imagine having all the money you want - **then** what qualities of things or experiences do you wish for? To attract money and enhance your well-being, focus on the things you believe you will get **from** having money.

 EXERCISE FOR YOU TO DO

What experiences or qualities do you want from having money?

EMPLOYMENT AND CAREER

Most people have natural talents, interests and abilities that come from the orientation of their soul. It is surely best to do what you love doing naturally.

Sometimes you have to move towards what you want and other times things just seem to seek you out!

 NOTE

Working just for money is poverty consciousness and wage

slavery. It is best to choose employment that is emotionally fulfilling to you **and** which pays well.

 EXERCISE FOR YOU TO DO

Exercise aim: to choose employment that is best for you.

Expected result: clarity about what you enjoy working at.

1   Write down **all** the ways you have earned money in the past.

2   Write down **all** the most interesting activities you have enjoyed, been involved in, or have done.

3   Are there ways to combine your answers to questions 1 and 2?

4   My best work/employment/career direction is ...

 KEY INSIGHT

☆   Follow what interests you the most, what gives you pleasure and what works best for you.

FAILURE AND SUCCESS

Oddly enough, there's not so much difference between the two.

Actually, there's nothing mysterious about how some people seem to achieve effortless success, while others achieve effortless failure. It's largely a question of attitude and application.

So here's some things to try, which might shed some light on this subject.

 EXERCISE FOR YOU TO DO

Make some notes beginning:

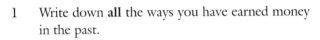

"The things I regard I have succeeded in achieving in my life so far include ..."

"The things I regard I have failed to achieve in my life so far include ..."

 VIEWPOINTS

★ Success and failure are relative to the perceptions you place on events and actions.

☆ Success is an objective emotion.

★ Success is easiest built up in steps.

"There is no scent like success."   Elizabeth Taylor

 EXERCISE FOR YOU TO DO

Let's continue to explore your own successes and failures a bit more.

Do you have more successes, or more failures?

When you review your life up to this point, which category - success or failure - do you consider you have given more attention and focus to?

How do you perceive and evaluate your successes?

How do you perceive and evaluate your failures?

 KEY INSIGHT

☆ Fear of failure - or indeed fear of success - can influence and determine what is achieved or not achieved.

Which do you fear the more: failure or success?

If you could allow no past failures or adverse circumstances to influence you **now** in achieving something you want, what would it be?

If there were no obstacles to achieving your next goal successfully, what is there to prevent you starting it **now**?

 KEY INSIGHTS

★   Sometimes opportunities for success arrive disguised in ordinary "clothes".

☆   Opportunities come more quickly when you are prepared to meet them.

CHAPTER 6.4

WELFARE, HEALTH AND ENVIRONMENT

Personal welfare can include your levels of health, happiness and general well-being, and these overlap with what we have already introduced in earlier chapters.

Generally speaking, the welfare of any individual or group of people is determined by

1   the amount of personal power an individual possesses and their ability to create what they require and desire

2   self-beliefs

3   specific beliefs about the influence of personal circumstances and the quality of experiences related to these factors

4   the role of government, the use of civil liberties and rights, and social responsibilities towards other people.

 EXERCISE FOR YOU TO DO

Write down some reflections.

Do you experience good levels of well-being and positive general welfare in your life?

What factors determine your welfare?

What do you believe about these factors?

HEALTH

Health is a vastly intricate and involved topic to be specific about, because every individual is both unique and different. Medical science has not adequately established a complete understanding of what comprises "health" and what is "normal", because there is a multitude of factors that contribute towards, and determine, levels of health experienced by anyone at any one time.

In the past, medical advice about health matters usually consisted, and still does to some extent, of lists of dos and don'ts - which seemed to change from time to time. Happily, in recent times, preventive attitudes in medicine have gained much credibility, but sometimes it still seems that too much is spent on drugs and the alleviation of symptoms, and not enough on health promotion and the eradication of causes. In the meantime, the NHS budget increases inexorably.

The views of modern medical science have changed, and now encompass a more complex view of health: from being entirely based on the human body, towards including mind, emotions **and** beliefs. A more holistic approach to health is beginning to emerge.

The magic and influence of belief and attitude upon the body, and the health and recovery of a patient has, in the history of Western culture at least, been greatly underestimated. Certain beliefs held in the subconscious mind can hold the power of life and death, and can determine the underlying cause of many, but not all, health problems.

No one would say, of course, that accident and emergency medical procedures should not be used when needed. But there are other maladies that may respond to the healing treatment of the emotions and beliefs. Perhaps the natural life-force that designed and built our bodies from one cell knows best how to repair and maintain it, if appropriately assisted and allowed to.

 EXERCISE FOR YOU TO DO

Make some notes.

My beliefs about my state of health are ...

My health problems (if any) are ...

I believe these health problems may be caused by ...

KEY INSIGHT

★ The gift of life is the most valuable of all.

ENVIRONMENT

Much has been said and written about Green and environmental issues over the past decade or two - particularly issues around pollution and overexploitation.

It's not enough just to examine the effects of pollution; we need also to look at the causes. These must exist within the belief systems, attitudes and behaviours of those who create the pollution. All of us, to some extent, are the originators because we all use transport, fuels, chemicals, papers etc.

If these beliefs and attitudes change, then the long-term relationship we all have with the environment will be much healthier.

 EXERCISE FOR YOU TO DO

Time now to make some more notes to yourself.

My beliefs about the quality of our environment are ...

What I believe about who is responsible for this is ...

What I believe I can do to assist matters is ...

SECTION 7
CONCLUSION AND REVIEW

7.1 CONCLUSION
7.2 REVIEW OF KEY INSIGHTS
7.3 SUGGESTED ADDITIONAL READING
7.4 SOME FURTHER RECOMMENDATIONS OF
     THINGS TO DO

*I have the key
to my life's
experiences.*

CHAPTER 7.1

CONCLUSION

This diagram represents a complete summary of the contents of this book.
If you use it well, you may be successful
in having the life you want!

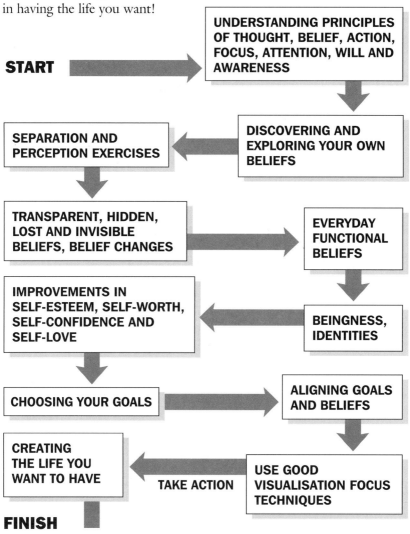

REVIEW OF KEY INSIGHTS

Here are the key insights again that occur throughout this book. Use this chapter as a quick-find review and summary whenever you feel you want or need a refresher.

 ALL KEY INSIGHTS

☆ There is a difference between thought and belief.

★ Your most important beliefs are those that are held with feelings.

☆ People create things with their thoughts. Thoughts can be entertained, modified or acted upon. Any thought, concept or idea constantly held in the mind (or believed in) becomes a belief.

★ **For every effect there is a cause.**

☆ **It is logical to suggest that for every effect (experience, event or creation) you have in your life, there is some cause responsible for it (arising from your thoughts, beliefs or actions).**

★ People can change their thoughts and actions easily enough, but the beliefs that have the real power that govern their lives, which are often held deep in their mind, are usually out of their everyday awareness, and are not necessarily easily found, accessed or changed.

☆ It is not just the range and quality of beliefs a person may hold, but the ones they choose to act on the most, that become the most significant.

★ The beliefs people hold and the actions they take with these beliefs determine the circumstances and quality of their lives.

☆ Quality thoughts and beliefs lead to quality life experiences!

★ Most persistent or personal problems are either created or influenced by beliefs containing some form of powerlessness.

★ The reality caused by the use of power in society is the existence of either domination or submission between individuals or groups of people. However, power can be shared!

☆ A person can have any number of beliefs, of any nature, arranged in any order of importance.

★ Your beliefs are stored in your subconscious mind.

☆ It is not just **what** a person believes that matters, but **how** they believe it.

★ A person's beliefs tend to affect each other and affect how they function together.

☆ The number, nature, structure and arrangement of a person's beliefs will determine what they create and what they experience.

★ The belief systems at the core of our being create the energy centres (or chakras) which govern our bodies and our lives. These chakras hold patterns of consciousness; therefore, whoever sees the world in terms of love and compassion will create that reality with their belief system.

☆ The arrangement or alignment of any individual or set of beliefs is as important as the nature of those beliefs. For every belief can affect the role of any other belief.

★ The kinds of beliefs a person holds may **not** lead them in the direction of achieving goals or desires, but away from them!

☆ Without fundamental belief change, any effort used to change your life may not be successful or long-lasting. When your key beliefs remain unchanged, you are likely to experience a return to similar circumstances, or to have repetitive life-experience patterns.

★ You **are** aware will.

☆ Your will rules all - it can determine belief creation and viewpoint.

★ Your mind can influence your body (and emotions) and your body can influence your mind.

☆ **BELIEFS CREATE YOUR OUTER REALITY.**

★ **BELIEFS CAUSE EXPERIENCE.**

☆ **BELIEFS PRECEDE (COME OR EXIST BEFORE) EXPERIENCE.**

★ To experience something as it truly is, is to be present with one's perceptions without expectation, judgement or definition.

☆ Truth is only relative to the point of view from which it is perceived ... because what you look **at,** and where you look **from,** determine your perception of what truth is.

★ Deciding **what** you want to believe is the **fundamental** aspect of creating what you want in life.

☆ Personal reality reflects what a person truly believes - which is not always the same as what they may be pretending or wanting to believe.

★ Existence is ...

☆ And ...

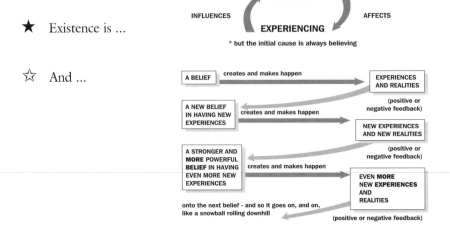

☆ And so ...

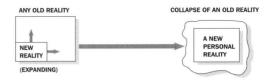

★ **Create with the flow of life.**

☆ **ALL BELIEFS FUNCTION IN PRESENT TIME ...**

... even if they are about the past or the **future.**

★ **In the present moment you have the power to choose your thoughts, beliefs and actions. If you have a present-time existence, you have a future.**

☆ Beliefs about reality create how reality is experienced.

★ Some limitations to the realities we experience are self-created and self-imposed.

☆ You cannot have or maintain **any** creation or experience unless you possess enough relative self-belief to sustain it.

★ Source awareness creates or empowers **any** identity, self-belief or collection of beliefs imposed on it.

☆ Source **awareness** plus **definition** equals **identity.**

★ All **definitions** of self, identity or being are all products of belief, usually characterised by "**I am ...**" beliefs.

☆ All identities and selves contain sets of beliefs that are **more** influential than **most** other forms of belief because they are of a higher order. That is, they are more important and stronger.

★ Each identity or self has its own set of beliefs.

☆ Some identities or selves **conflict** with each other, whilst others **reinforce** each other.

★ Identities and selves are either ...

asserted - what you want to be, or

resisted - what you don't want to be.

★ Contradictions and conflicts within an identity or self tend to neutralise each other.

☆ Identities can only be changed by the original creator. So, the key is to work to get the persistent identities to entertain change or transformation.

★ By teaching identities how to change and build new belief structures, **resistant** identities can be evolved into **deliberate** identities, and greater flexibility achieved in one's state of being.

☆ **Identifying** and **raising** one's self-beliefs that contain the lowest or most negative levels of self-esteem is the best way to raise the overall, or average, level of self-esteem.

★ Improving the lowest or weakest part of your self-beliefs will influence and lift all the other parts.

☆ Hidden and invisible beliefs are characterised by these factors:

1   they tend to be totally and unquestionably true to the believer

2   they tend to be the beliefs you take for granted

3   the proof for holding a hidden or invisible belief is actually **produced** by the belief itself.

★ Keep holding your visualisations and visions - but let things happen naturally!

☆ There is always a time delay in creating your goal - be patient!

★ When your goals and beliefs are in alignment, life unfolds and things happen at the right time!

☆ You can allow yourself to be happy - for no reason at all! Happiness is not something you have to earn, deserve, work for or pay for.

Happiness and fulfilment naturally come from the inside of your being when there is an absence of resistance or negativity ... this is why in the long term it is difficult to sustain a source of happiness if it depends only on someone or something outside of yourself.

☆ It is common to believe that money can solve all your problems and automatically provide the experiences you desire. However, imagine having all the money you want - **then** what qualities of things or experiences do you wish for? To attract money and enhance your well-being, focus on the things you believe you will get **from** having money.

★ Follow what interests you the most, what gives you pleasure and what works best for you.

☆ Fear of failure - or indeed fear of success - can influence and determine what is achieved or not achieved.

★ Sometimes opportunities for success arrive disguised in ordinary "clothes".

☆ Opportunities come more quickly when you are prepared to meet them.

★ The gift of life is the most valuable of all.

 FUNDAMENTAL INSIGHT

YOU EXPERIENCE WHAT YOU BELIEVE!

THEREFORE THE FUTURE SURVIVAL OF HUMANKIND INVOLVES THE DEVELOPMENT AND USE OF BELIEFS.

 **CONCLUSION**

SO **WHAT** DO YOU BELIEVE?

AND **WHAT** DO YOU EXPERIENCE?

SUGGESTED ADDDITIONAL READING

Creating money, Sanaya Roman and Duane Packer. H J Kramer, USA 1988, £9.99. ISBN 0 915 81109 X

Heal your body, Louise Hay. Eden Grove Editions, London 1982, £3.99. ISBN 1 870845 04 8

Jitterbug perfume, Tom Robbins. Bantam Books 1991. ISBN 0 553 403834
A novel about beliefs, experiences, and immortality!

Men are from Mars, women are from Venus, John Gray. Thorsons 1993, £8.99. ISBN 0 7225 2840 X
See also other titles.

Moneylove, Jerry Gillies. Warner Books 1978, £4.99. ISBN 0 446 35379 5

Recreating yourself, Christopher Stove. Napier, USA. ISBN 0 393312 43 7

The path to love, Deepak Chopra. Rider Books, London 1997, £9.99. ISBN 0 7126 7224 9

The power is within you, Louise Hay. Eden Grove Editions, London 1991, £8.99. ISBN 1 870845 10 2

The power of your subconscious mind, Dr Joseph Murphy. Simon & Schuster Ltd, London 1963, £7.99. ISBN 0 671 85460 7
This one is recommended reading.

The way of the wizard, Deepak Chopra. Rider Books, London 1996, £9.99. ISBN 0 7126 7207 9

CHAPTER 7.4

SOME FURTHER RECOMMENDATIONS OF THINGS TO DO

Any course that specialises in beliefs and belief awareness.

Belief counselling.*

Any of the large number of relaxation, stress management, awareness or meditation techniques available today, and applications to affect the subconscious mind.

Hypnotherapy.

Floating in a flotation tank.

Conscious connected relaxation breathing (otherwise called kriya yoga, rebirthing, vivation or chakra breathing).

*Belief counselling talks, courses and trainings are available. Please contact the author at the publisher's address:

Seven Stars Publishing
2 The Esplanade
The Hoe
Plymouth PL1 2PJ
phone and fax 01752 269555

Further titles to follow.

NOTES

NOTES